Dependent Personality Disorder

Cognitive behavioral therapy self-help guide

What are personality disorders, treatment, signs, symptoms, CBT techniques, all covered

By James Frank

Published by Cleal Publishing

Copyright ©2016 Cleal Publishing

ISBN (978-0-9955610-0-7)

Disclaimer

While the author and publisher have made all available efforts to ensure the information contained in this book was correct at press time, neither the author nor publisher assume and hereby disclaim any liability to any party for damages, disruption, or loss caused by the use and application, directly or indirectly, of any information presented including any errors. This book is not meant to substitute medical advice from a qualified healthcare professional. The reader should regularly consult with a healthcare professional in matters relating to his/her mental health and particularly with respect to any of the symptoms discussed which may require professional treatment.

We have no control over the nature, content, and availability of the web sites listed in this book. The inclusion of any web site links does not necessarily imply a recommendation or endorse the views expressed within them. Cleal Publishing takes no responsibility for, and will not be liable for, the websites being temporarily unavailable or being removed from the internet.

The accuracy and completeness of information provided herein and opinions stated herein are not guaranteed or warranted to produce any particular results, and the advice and strategies, contained herein may not be suitable for every individual.

Acknowledgements

Thank you to my lovely daughter for putting up with my writing habit.

Contents

Chapter One: Introduction

Have you ever struggled with feelings of inadequacy? Depression? Anxiety? If so, you are not alone. There are literally millions of people out there who suffer from the same symptoms. That said, this book is designed to give you some tangible steps you can use not only to recognize your symptoms, but also to integrate techniques and exercises to overcome them.

This book will introduce you to the world of cognitive behavioral therapy. This is the approach I am going to use to show you how you can make changes to your thinking and behavior that can help you manage life's adversities. That said, the first part will assume a more professional style so as to introduce you to common conditions, their symptoms, and treatments. Once you have that information I will focus more on addressing you personally, and focusing on what you can do to identify dependent personality disorder and manage your problems at home.

Throughout this book, two case studies will be integrated to give you a better understanding of the practices and techniques in real life.

The two case studies follow one male, Michael, and one female, Heather.

These two individuals suffer from dependent personality disorder.

Michael is a forty-year-old man who is currently having marital difficulties. He finds his marriage unsatisfying because his wife doesn't spend much time with him as she spends a lot of time developing her business. He struggles to express this dissatisfaction with his wife, as the thought of doing so leaves him anxious and worried that she will leave him. Over the last decade, Michael stayed at home looking after the children but now that his children have left for college, he has not built up a career and feels inadequate as a result, leaving him scared about taking steps toward getting back into the work place. This has resulted in him putting it off for months.

Heather is a thirty-five-year-old woman who is stuck in a dead-end job. She is continually passed over for a promotion due to her inability to initiate projects without constant reassurance from all of her colleagues. She is anxious about making everybody happy but, as a result, she fails to voice her discontent over certain policies and people in the workplace.

Chapter Two: Mental Health and Personality Disorders

Personality disorder has been defined as "enduring patterns of inner experience and behaviors that deviate markedly from the expectations of the individual's culture, is pervasive and inflexible…is stable over time, and leads to distress or impairment" (American Psychiatric Association, 2013, p. 645).

Mental health professional use either the Diagnostic and Statistical Manual of Mental Disorders (American Psychiatric Association, 2013) or the International Classification of Mental and Behavioural Disorders (ICD-10) to diagnose mental health problems.

Mental health problems frequently go undiagnosed and therefore untreated, causing ongoing misery. With this in mind, it can be useful to learn about these common conditions to help develop an understanding for yourself whether you may be suffering from an undiagnosed problem. Only a qualified healthcare professional can properly diagnose conditions, but the following information could help you raise concerns with your doctor for further investigation if appropriate.

The disorders listed below list a range of common anxiety problems.

Generalized Anxiety Disorder	:	A disorder related to extreme worry and anxiety that impacts how people feel physically (muscle tension, restless, fatigue, sleeping problems, irritability, and difficulties with concentration).
Post-Traumatic Stress Disorder	:	Also known as PTSD; occurs in someone due to an extreme traumatic event such as rape, combat, disaster,

		road traffic accident, etc. Symptoms include nightmares and flashbacks.
Obsessive-Compulsive Disorder	:	Affecting about 3 per cent of the world population, OCD, as it is also known, involves experiencing recurrent intrusive thoughts (obsessions) and repetitive behaviors (compulsions).
Phobias	:	Fear or anxiety of an object or situation.
Panic Disorder	:	Characterized by a rush of physical symptoms accompanied by fear and frightening thoughts of disaster, e.g., feeling lightheaded and interpreting this sensation as indication that one is about to pass out.
Social Anxiety Disorder	:	Sometimes regarded as social phobia where one has a fear of embarrassing oneself in a social situation.

Mood Disorder

This is a type of disorder that relates to extreme changes of moods. Types of this disorder are:

Bipolar Disorder	:	Also known as manic depression, as the patient of this disorder will suffer from at least one manic behavior, i.e., very hyper activities. There may also be mood swings.
Cyclothymic Disorder	:	Severe mood shifts but less serious than bipolar conditions.
Depression	:	Extreme feeling of sadness causing difficulty to go about leading life normally.

Personality Disorders

Personality disorders represent a range of conditions that affect people in very different ways. However, they generally tend to negatively affect the individuals' relationships with others and can cause profound distress. Below are some descriptions of the different types of personality disorder.

Paranoid Personality Disorder

Those with paranoid personality disorder have an unjustified mistrust and suspiciousness of others (American Psychiatric Association, 2013). They tend to hold negative core beliefs about other people, with the theme of others being out to cause them harm or take advantage of them. It is understandable, therefore, that they often feel anxious around other people and are careful of sharing information about themselves with others. They tend to persistently doubt the trustworthiness of people they come into contact with and they therefore understandably struggle to build relationships with others.

Schizoid Personality Disorder

People with schizoid personality disorder are generally seen as "loners" – they lack social connections and often are not interested in sexual relationships. It does not bother them that they don't have many significant relationships with others. They sometimes appear to others as being chilly. They feel indifferent to interpersonal relationships and struggle to express emotions (American Psychiatric Association, 2013). They tend to choose to engage in solitary activities and when around others and may appear withdrawn.

Schizotypal Personality Disorder

Individuals with schizotypal personality disorder have a decreased potential for closeness with others and feel very uncomfortable with close relationships (American Psychiatric Association, 2013). They experience a lot of anxiety when in social situations and may hold the belief that they are different from others. They struggle to form relationships. They experience unusual perceptual experiences such as hallucinations. They may hold firmly to odd beliefs that lack everyday logic. They may link events without any plausible connection in the form of magical thinking. People may view them as odd or eccentric due to their unusual behavior.

Anti-Social Personality Disorder

People with anti-social personality disorder demonstrate criminal behavior, impulsiveness, and aggression and are irresponsible

(American Psychiatric Association, 2013). They lack any care for the suffering of other people that may result from their behavior. They may be vulnerable to drug/alcohol misuse and impulsive or risky behavior. Their relationships with other people tend to be shallow and they can exploit others for their own benefit.

Borderline Personality Disorder

The phrase "borderline" was coined by Adolph Strict in 1938. It was used to explain clients who were on a "borderline" between neurosis and psychosis.

Individual with this difficulty act impulsively and are emotionally unstable (American Psychiatric Association, 2013). Often they will experience episodes of intense emotion and emotional outbursts, including anger. They may hold the belief that they are defective or vulnerable (Sperry & Sperry, 2016). Their relationships with others tend to be unstable. Due to their struggling to regulate their emotions and tolerate distress, they may engage in high-risk behaviors, such as self-harm or suicidal gestures. They may have an unstable self of sense in terms of their identity (Cowen et al., 2012).

Histrionic Personality Disorder

Individuals with histrionic personality disorder show a routine of extreme emotionality and attention-seeking behavior (American Psychiatric Association, 2013). They show an extreme need for acceptance by others. They are likely to behave dramatically and can be inappropriately flirtatious with others. They may hold beliefs about the need to be attached to others due to viewing themselves as inadequate (Sungur & Gündüz, 2015).

Narcissistic Personality Disorder

The phrase "narcissistic personality disorder" was first used by Heinz Kohut in 1971 to describe clients who have a special feeling of self-importance and a hunger for appreciation.

They will tend to inflate their self-esteem and struggle with empathy (American Psychiatric Association, 2013). People with narcissistic personality disorder often appear "larger than life" and embellish their achievements.

However, they also have a very delicate self-esteem and believe that they are defective in some way, which leaves them feeling that they are undesirable to others.

A narcissistic individual's job performance may also suffer from the problem. They struggle to accept criticism from other people, which can mean they have difficulties working well with others.

Avoidant Personality Disorder

Individuals with avoidant personality disorder struggle with regularly feeling inadequate, and constantly worried about what other people think of them. They expect to be rejected by others, leaving them feeling extreme anxiety in social situations when it comes to building relationships with others (Padesky & Beck, 2015).

People with this problem regularly consider themselves to be individually unpleasant and inferior to other people. They will often avoid social interaction leave them feeling lonely. In contrast to schizoid personality disorder, those with avoidant personality disorder would ideally like to have relationships with others but are inhibited by their anxiety.

Obsessive-compulsive Personality Disorder

Clients with obsessive-compulsive personality disorder struggle with unhelpful perfectionism and orderliness (American Psychiatric Association, 2013). Other people may view them as rigid and stubborn. They strive to achieve unrelenting high standards in the areas of performance and achievement. Achieving their high standards is prioritized over relaxation and enjoyment of life.

They may hold beliefs about being responsible for everything but also being inadequate (Sperry & Sperry, 2016). They over compensate for these beliefs by exerting a high level of control over their behavior. Many end up being workaholics leaving them exhausted. They put all their eggs in one basket, so to speak, by placing extreme importance in doing well in one or two aspects of their life such as work or sports. This leaves them vulnerable to depression and anxiety when things don't go perfectly well in these areas or they receive negative feedback.

Symptoms Associated with Dependent Personality Disorder

Individuals with dependent personality disorder are afraid of separating or being left by significant people in their lives, which can cause needy behavior. This behavior can leave the individual at risk of being used by others.

As individuals with dependent personality disorder need continuous support, they may struggle to make decisions or to finish projects on their own.

They often put themselves down and avoid disagreeing with others even when they know the person is incorrect.

Dependent personality disorder is a pervasive fear that results in clinging behavior in early adulthood, whereby those affected have difficulty making normal decisions throughout their daily lives without constant and excessive reassurance from others and advice from others (American Psychiatric Association, 2013). Anxiety and depression are key symptoms associated with this disorder, which manifest in everyday life.

Dependent personality disorder often brings with it feelings of self-doubt and pessimism, both of which belittle the assets and abilities of the individual. Disapproval or criticism is taken as proof of being worthless, which is why many people will seek dominance and overprotection from other people. In return, the individual will become dependent and submissive, out of fear that they cannot live without help from others.

An individual with dependent personality disorder will face difficulty making everyday decisions, will need other people to take responsibility for the major areas of their life, will not express disagreement with others, and will not start projects or do things on their own. Individuals will also feel uncomfortable if they are left alone and will go to great lengths to get the support they need from others. They remain unrealistically preoccupied with the fear of having to take care of themselves.

Given that such disorders revolve around long-term behavioral patterns, most personality disorders, including dependent personality disorder, are diagnosed in adulthood.

Those who suffer from dependent personality disorder often deal with secondary symptoms, which include depression, anxiety, and difficulties adjusting to life changes.

Depression

Depression includes excessive emotions of unhappiness over an extended period, often for more than a few weeks or months.

- Depressed people are often regarded as weak or lazy;
- Social stigma causes people to avoid the treatment they need;
- The symptoms suffered by the person are so disabling that they are often unable to seek help;

- Many of the symptoms are misdiagnosed as physical problems.

Psychological Symptoms

Typical emotional warning signs of depressive disorders include:

- Lack of motivation
- Continuous low mood or sadness
- Feeling irritable and intolerant of others
- Lack of enjoyment in previously enjoyable activities
- Feeling anxious or worried
- Low self-esteem
- Feelings of helplessness and hopelessness
- Difficulty in making decisions
- Suicidal thoughts
- Reduced sex drive
- Feelings of guilt
- Tearfulness

Physical Symptoms

Typical physical symptoms of depression include:

- Change in appetite and weight loss or weight gain
- Lack of energy
- Slowed movement or speech
- Changes to the menstrual cycle (in women)
- Constipation
- Lack of interest in sex
- Unexplained aches and pains

Social Symptoms

Typical social symptoms of depression include:

- Reduced contact with friends
- Less interest in hobbies and activities
- Decrease in performance at work
- Difficulties in home and family life
- Taking part in fewer social activities

Depression is a mood disorder wherein feelings of frustration, loss, sadness, or anger will interfere with daily life for a period of weeks or more. Major depressive disorder (MDD) is a mental disorder characterized by low self-esteem and low mood alongside a lack of pleasure in regular activities. MDD will change or otherwise distort the manner in which an individual sees themselves, their lives, or the people around them. It will cause individuals to view things through a negative prism.

Certain types of clinical depression are thought to be hereditary, but it can occur without any family history of depression. Major depressive disorder will adversely affect the general health, family, work life, school life, sleeping habits, and eating habits of the individual. It can sometimes lead to suicide if left untreated.

The most common treatment includes psychotherapy or counseling alone or in combination with anti-depressant medication.

Causes

There are three types of causes for MDD including biological, psychological, and social. It is assumed that depression is the result of vulnerability according to the diathesis-stress model, which can be activated during stressful periods in life. This vulnerability can be genetic or schematic. As a result, different people respond to different stressful life events in various ways, based on their ability to cope with these stressful life events.

The monoamine hypothesis states that researchers have linked clinical depression to the function of three neurochemicals: serotonin, dopamine, and norepinephrine.

If an individual is subject to decreased serotonin levels, it may promote low levels of norepinephrine, which is related to energy, anxiety, alertness, attention, and an overall interest in life. Dopamine controls interest in life, reward, pleasure, attention, and motivation.

Another theory encompasses the brain structure. Neuroimaging studies have shown that those individuals who suffer from clinical depression had an increased volume of the adrenal gland and lateral ventricles as well as smaller volumes of the frontal lobe, thalamus, hippocampus, and basal ganglia. With a loss of hippocampus neurons, individuals may be more prone to depression, dysthymic mood, and impaired memory.

There are many outside factors that can affect and/or cause depression including the following:

Substance abuse

Comorbid medical conditions, especially those associated with chronic pain

Persistent insomnia

Medication side effects

Stressful life events and losses

Symptoms

The symptoms of clinical major depression (MMD) include:

- Depressed mood
- Loss of interest in all or most activities
- Insomnia
- Low energy
- Poor concentration
- Change in appetite
- Change in weight
- Thoughts of guilt or worthlessness
- Psychomotor agitation or retardation
- Recurrent thoughts about suicide or death

The aforementioned symptoms can be grouped into three disturbances:

Emotions (a loss of interest or depressed mood)

Ideation (feelings of guilt, worthlessness, thoughts of suicide or death)

Somatic or fatigued symptoms (energy, concentration, psychomotor, appetite, weight, sleep)

Adjustment disorders are a form of reactive depression, which takes place once an individual is unable to cope for an extended period with a major change in life that causes stress. This means that difficulty coping with life stressors can lead to it. For those who are psychologically stable before experiencing an injury, daily normal routines can become overwhelming and lead to depression.

Treatment (Pharmacological, Psychological Therapy)

Basic treatment may include either medication in the form of antidepressants or psychotherapy. For more severe cases, the treatment includes a combination of medication and psychotherapy.

The most common medications include SSRI's or SNRI's:

SSRI:

Selective serotonin reuptake inhibitors. The most popular medications include Prozac (fluoxetine), Zoloft (sertraline), Paxil (paroxetine), Luvox (fluvoxamine), Celexa (citalopram), and Lexapro (escitalopram).

SNRI:

Serotonin-norepinephrine reuptake inhibitors. The most popular of these medications include Pristiq (desvenlafaxine), Effexor (venlafaxine), and Cymbalta (duloxetine).

Other medications also include tricyclic antidepressants, monoamine oxidase inhibitors (MAOIs), Wellbutrin (bupropion, blocks reuptake of norepinephrine and dopamine), and Remeron (mirtazapine).

There are two types of talking therapy that have a strong evidence base for their effectiveness in treating depression:

- Cognitive behavioral therapy: this teaches the individual how to manage the key symptoms of depression such as negative thinking patterns and changes in behavior that might unintentionally maintain the problem. This therapy also includes teaching problem-solving skills.

- Behavioral activation: this teaches the individual how to overcome depression by engaging in important and rewarding activities. There is a particular focus on identifying and making changes to patterns of avoidance behaviors (Veale & Willson, 2007).

Other treatment methods include electroconvulsive therapy. This is an effective treatment for severe cases of depression. Transcranial magnetic stimulation uses energy pulses to stimulate nerve cells located in the brain responsible for controlling the mood.

Anxiety

A little anxiety is good, and we all experience it at times. But a little stress becomes detrimental when it manifests in the form of anxiety. Anxiety can interfere with your capability to focus and sleep, as well as affecting your appetite. Anxiety and anxiety disorder are among the most commonly handled issues in therapy.

Anxiety is a coping mechanism to secure the body against danger or stress. Hormones, such as adrenalin, are released, causing the heart to beat faster to bring blood where it is needed most. Your respiration accelerates to bring the oxygen necessary for energy and sweating begins to cool the body. This allows the system to secure itself in dangerous situations by either running away or fighting a foe – the "fight or flight" response.

To cope with anxiety, some individuals may start smoking, drinking or misusing drugs; others may avoid social situations or worry excessively.

Some of the warning signs of anxiety disorder include:

- Generalized emotions of tension and fear in circumstances where there is no real cause for concern or where the anxiety signs are out of proportion.
- Obsessive ideas and behaviors

- Panic attacks
- Phobias

Controlling the Warning Signs of Anxiety

The warning signs of anxiety can be controlled by some behavioral techniques. Regular exercise, which uses up adrenalin and testosterone made because of stress, and avoiding motivators such as alcohol, coffee, and cigarettes may also be beneficial.

Medication such as SSRI's (selective this reuptake inhibitors) or beta-blockers may be prescribed to deal with the warning signs of tension.

Many people benefit from seeing a qualified healthcare professional who has been trained in CBT.

Use of CBT to Treat Anxiety

The focus of CBT is to help individuals find the links between their thoughts and anxiety. Therapy often progresses through a series of steps:

Step 1

Teaching clients to concretely identify the thoughts, images, predictions, interpretations, and beliefs that create anxiety

Step 2

Teaching clients to treat their thoughts as hypothesis rather than "fact"

Step 3

Encouraging clients to gather "evidence" for and against these hypotheses

Step 4

Examining evidence to determine if the client's original thought is accurate

Step 5

Compiling a range of realistic alternative interpretations that cause the client less anxiety

Step 6

Teaching the client to choose the least anxiety-provoking self-statement that is believable and use it to replace the original anxiety-provoking statement.

Step 7

If the alternative self-statement does not work, encouraging the client to try a different one.

The overall aim for CBT in this sense is to allow the client to develop a more balanced realistic perspective.

Things to Remember

- Those with paranoid personality issue have an unjustified mistrust and doubts of others. They worry that others are taking advantage of or misleading them. A simple claim may be regarded as a danger or an attack on their personality.
- People with schizoid personality problem are generally seen as "loners" – they lack social connections and often do not get married. They sometimes appear to others as being chilly and unsociable.
- Clients with schizotypal personality disorder have a decreased potential for closeness with others that exists from a young age. They often have altered or unusual beliefs and behaviors that can cause them appear odd.
- People with anti-social personality disorder appear to feel a restricted variety of emotions. Clients with the problem may be vulnerable to drug misuse or risky behavior as a technique of trying to evade their feelings of loneliness.
- Clients with histrionic character problem show a routine of extreme emotionality and attention-seeking behavior.
- People with narcissistic personality disorder often embellish their achievements. However, they also have a very delicate self-esteem and believe that they are defective in some way.
- Clients with avoidant personality disorder struggle with regularly feeling inadequate, and constantly worried about what other people think of them.
- Clients with obsessive-compulsive personality disorder are engaged with perfectionism and orderliness.
- An individual with dependent personality disorder will face difficulty making everyday decisions, will need other people to take responsibility for the major areas of their life, will not express disagreement with others, and will not start projects or do things on their own. Individuals will also feel uncomfortable if they are left alone and will go to great

lengths to get the support they need from others. They remain unrealistically preoccupied with the fear of having to take care of themselves.

- Depression is a clinical mood disorder wherein feelings of frustration, loss, sadness, or anger will interfere with daily life for weeks or more.
- Adjustment disorders are a form of reactive depression that takes place once an individual is unable to cope for an extended period to a major change in life that cases stress.
- Depression and anxiety can often go hand in hand. Anxiety is a coping mechanism to secure the body against danger or stress, but it can cause complications and sickness or even a lack of concentration.
- The warning signs of anxiety can be controlled by some behavioral techniques. Regular exercise, which uses up adrenalin and other testosterone made through stress and avoiding motivators such as alcohol, coffee, and cigarettes may also be beneficial.
- The overall aim for CBT in this sense is to allow the client to develop a more balanced perspective.

Chapter Three: How Common Are Personality Disorders?

The U.S. National Institute of Mental Health (NIMH) took a census of psychological disorders to determine how common said disorders were and to determine the answer to questions such as whether gender or ethnicity predisposes someone to the risk of having a specific disorder.

The results of this work estimate that 1 in 6 Americans suffers from an active disorder. Generalized anxiety manifested in 10.4% of men and 17.7% of women in America, and was seen at rates of 9.7% for whites, 23.4% for blacks, and 12.2% for Hispanics.

Perhaps more interesting is that the findings revealed that the serious psychological disorders presented at a rate twice as high for people below the poverty line (Centers for Disease Control, 1992) and with 75% of first symptoms presenting by age 24 (Robins & Regier, 1991, p. 656).

Studies indicate that there is a prevalence of between 0.4 and 1.5% of dependent personality disorder in the general population (Grant et al., 2004). Many of those with this disorder experience few symptoms as a child, but the severity of the symptoms increases with age and can last into their 40s and 50s.

CBT has changed the field of mental health profoundly over the last four decades by influencing the manner in which therapists work with individuals. Nearly half, roughly 49%, of all faculty among clinical psychology doctoral programs are focused on cognitive therapy or cognitive behavioral therapy (Mayne, 1994).

Things to Remember

- 1 in 6 Americans suffers from an active disorder.

- Generalized anxiety manifested in 10.4% of men and 17.7% of women in America, and was seen at rates of 9.7% for whites, 23.4% for blacks, and 12.2% for Hispanics.
- Serious psychological disorders presented at a rate twice as high for people below the poverty line (Centers for Disease Control, 1992) and with 75% of first symptoms presenting by age 24 (Robins & Regier, 1991, p. 656).
- Studies indicate that there is a prevalence of between 0.4 and 1.5% of dependent personality disorder in the general population.

Chapter Four: Using Cognitive Behavior Therapy to Help Yourself

Cognitive therapy assumes that the way a person thinks influences how that person feels and behaves. Events do not cause our emotions. Our emotional responses to events are influenced by our interpretations (thoughts) about these events. Overgeneralized explanations and self-blaming for events are a concrete part of the depression cycle, and people with depression might interpret suggestions as criticism, disagreement as dislike, friendliness as pity, and praise as flattery. By ruminating on these thoughts, individuals remain in a bad mood.

That being said, if the patterns of depression and such damaging thoughts are learned behaviors then it stands to reason that they can be unlearned as well.

Cognitive therapists have explored various ways to teach people more constructive ways of thinking so that they can change the way they react emotionally and the way they think about events in life.

What Is Aaron Beck's Cognitive Behavioral Therapy?

Aaron Beck noticed that many individuals who suffered with depression had recurrent negative thoughts pop into their minds. He viewed these thoughts as playing an important part in maintaining depression and thought that therapy should therefore focus on helping individuals answer these negative automatic thoughts.

Beck and his colleagues decided to form a new type of cognitive therapy that would reverse the catastrophizing beliefs that clients had about themselves, about their situations, and about their futures (Beck, 1979).

What Beck discovered was that depressed people often believed that their failures were entirely blamed on themselves while their successes were entirely the result of external circumstances.

That being said, cognitive therapists sought to combine reversing the self-defeating thoughts with behavioral changes to form what we know today as cognitive behavioral therapy. This therapy focuses on altering the way people act and think. It makes people more aware of the negative and often irrational thinking they have, replaces that thinking with new, realistic ways of thinking, and helps patients to practice more positive approaches in their everyday life.

After undergoing cognitive behavioral therapy, patients learn to notice and take personal credit for the good events in their lives and to avoid blaming themselves for bad events or overgeneralizing bad events.

Cognitive behavioral therapy and self-help can be used for problems associated with dependent personality (Beck et al., 2015).

What can a client anticipate in CBT treatment?

CBT treatment begins with an assessment that allows the therapist to get a clear understanding of the issues that the client is suffering from, their current situation, and the changes they want to make.

From the assessment comes a set of treatment goals that determine what the client would like to achieve by the end of treatment. The assessment also allows the therapist and client to work together to identify what may be maintaining the problems for which the client is seeking help. This logically feeds into a treatment plan that aims to disrupt these factors keeping problems going in the present.

Often the therapist will recommend an action plan for the client to try out between therapy appointments—these are essential because this is where most of the change occurs. The more practice people put in with the CBT techniques, the more progress they usually notice.

Another essential aspect of treatment is to monitor problems as they come up in people's daily life. This information can often provide useful information about the problem that can be used to help the client to make changes.

The last sessions are devoted to going over the methods the client is familiar with and the knowledge they have obtained, so that if there are any drawbacks after treatment finishes, they will have the abilities and information to deal with them.

Homework is a key part of CBT. In CBT, a major portion of the therapy takes place in people's daily life, where they practice the CBT strategies to work toward making important changes.

The overall aim of this practice is to take steps toward achieving important goals and to eliminate the client's dependency on the therapist.

For example, unless client practices the new techniques that they learn to handle the problems for which they are seeking help, they will not use them very well, and will probably not use them when they need them most.

Therefore, homework is useful, as already mentioned, if it provides clients with practice in the CBT strategies covered during the therapy appointment.

It allows them to put the abilities they have found into practice in real-life situations.

Individuals who are willing to do projects at home seem to get the most benefit from CBT.

For example, a lot of people who have depressive disorders say they don't want to perform actions until they feel more motivated. CBT may present them with a substitute perspective – that motivation follows action. Therefore, to feel more motivated, you have to engage in activities in your daily life despite a lack of motivation.

So homework assignments might involve planning activities that are important into a diary and following this plan regardless of how you feel at the time. Doing this often will help people get more out of life and reverse the cycle of depression.

Chapter Five: Preparing Yourself for Change

Many people feel as if they don't belong to this world. They think that the world really hates them. They actually regret that they were ever born into this world. This is simply because working hard and doing what is universally considered the "right" things in life don't always amount to anything tangible at all. But the reason not everyone sees the fruits of their labor is that they actually have not spent a lot of time thinking about what they want in life and setting realistic steps toward achieving those goals. They don't know where they are going and thus they remain stuck at the same place. The thing is that you can never get where you want to go if you have no idea where you want to go.

Consider this simple example: You want to go out on a Friday night but you don't know where. You don't have an idea of where you want to go and, as a result, you end up sitting around discontented because you don't know what you want but you know you want *it* now. In the end, you remain at home all Friday night because you never made a decision and thus were never able to go anywhere.

Having a goal in life is a very important thing. If you want to be successful in life—whether that success is figuring out what to do on the weekend or being a wealthy and powerful CEO—you need goals. You should set goals for all of the various things that you want in life.

By setting goals, you are actually choosing where you want to go. By having a good picture of where you are going, chances are that you will be able to achieve your ambitions in life. Why should you then set goals? We will look at a number of key reasons why you should have goals and how you will achieve them.

Setting Personal Goals

There are levels that you can always use to set up your goal. Many sociologists have created their own versions of the whole process that have made it decidedly more complicated but broadly, it all boils down to the three methods.

- The first thing that you should do is to create what is called the "big picture." This is also called the "strategic level," where you are not bothered by what happens in the next 10 days. You are more concerned with what you want to achieve in the next 10 years and beyond.
- The next level is to break down the strategic level into smaller targets that will be geared toward hitting the lifetime goals.
- Lastly, you should now start working hard to ensure that your goals are reached.

When you follow these steps, chances are that you will be happier in life as you achieve the goals that you have set. When you have these goals, you should realize that every single day really counts. You should be very careful not to give up on the path of achieving your dreams. Every day wasted will end up pushing the goals further away from you until you don't even remember them. We will now look at a number of key stages on how to define these goals well in order to achieve them.

Step 1: Setting strategic goals (lifetime goals)

This is basically the stage where you take time to critically think about the things that you want to achieve over the years. It is the stage in which you want to decide who you want to be in life. When you have this strategic aspect to your goal setting, then there are chances that you will be very good in terms of your planning and goal setting.

There are many categories that you can decide to divide your goals into, all of which are important. When you set up goals in these categories, you will be at a good place to figure out how to accomplish them. It will give you a good perspective on the details that you want to have in your lifetime. Some of the categories that you come up with can include:

- Career—This is where you think in terms of your career and what you want to achieve in the process.
- Financial—You should think of the amount of money that you need to achieve your goals.
- Education—This is very important, as it will help you with the two above. Which course do you want to take in the future and which school do you want to attend?
- Family—In your goal setting, you should never forget your family. What kind of person do you want to marry? How many kids do you want to have?
- Artistic—If you are interested in art, you should ask yourself whether you want to achieve any goal artistically.
- Attitude—The kind of attitude that you have is very significant: Do you want to change some attitude or gain new ones? For instance, if you are always negative, you should have a goal that will explain to you how you want to change that.
- Physical—You should consider how you want to change in terms of physical features. In the process, you should consider whether you want to be fit or remain as you are.
- Pleasure—You also don't want a boring life. You want a life that you will enjoy as each day and night passes. Therefore, it is important to consider ways that you want to enjoy yourself.
- Public service—Do you want to improve life in your community or around the world?

There are many goals that you can have in life. As you create these goals, you should think of a bunch of ideas about what you want to achieve. Be careful not to leave out any of them. In each category, you should add as many points about what you want to achieve as possible. The goals should, however, be very realistic. In addition, these goals should come from you alone. You don't want to use goals that your parents, spouse, or significant other wants to achieve. That would be like living a life that is not yours. If you want to be a model and your father wants you to be a lawyer, you should realize that you only live once. You should follow what is fundamentally important to you.

Step 2: Setting smaller and short-term goals

After you have done the above, it is time to set smaller goals that you want to achieve in, say, the next five years or so. These will be the foundation or the so-called "building blocks" of the long-term strategic goals.

With these, you can continue to divide the plans in terms of one-year, six-month, one-month, and daily plans. These goals should be aligned to the achievement of the long-term goals. Say, for instance, you want to be a lawyer in the future. In that case, it is important for you to focus on your education and pass every exam that will be required in the whole process.

You should then create a checklist or the to-do-list of the things you want to do on a daily basis that are geared to the long-term goals.

One common mistake that you should never make is postponing things. For instance, when you come up with a brilliant idea of what you want to achieve, you should implement it as soon as possible. When you are postponing your dream, what you are doing is shifting your dream.

It is also very important to conduct reviews of the things that you want to achieve and whether you are achieving them. These could be done monthly or quarterly.

Staying on course

The next thing on which you should focus is the best way to achieve the goals that you have set. As soon as you have created a set of the goals that you want to achieve, you should keep on reviewing and updating the to-do-list on a regular basis. Though this could be a bit boring, you should know that it will help you a great deal with building a life worth living. You can use a book, notebook or a computer-based application.

Setting goals for change

The thing is that every Tom, Dick, and Harry can create a goal. However, only a small group of people can comfortably achieve their goals. The biggest problem in all this is that they set up goals that are not smart. It is always important to use the method of goal setting through the principle of SMART. This principle stands for the following:

S – Specific (the goal should be very specific)

M – Measurable (the goal can be measured and conceptualized)

A – Attainable (the goal should be something within reach)

R – Relevant (the goal should be rewarding)

T – Time-bound (the goal should have the time aspect integrated into it)

A good example of a SMART goal is: "I want to tour Africa in five months' time." This goal is both specific (Africa), measurable, attainable, relevant, and time-bound (in five months' time); the thing is that this could be a bit complicated if you did not have the time aspect.

There are a number of other tips that you should always think about when setting valid goals in life. Some of these tips are explained below:

- Always state the goal in a positive manner. Don't say that you don't want to make mistakes. Simply say what you want instead.
- When setting goals, always state something precise. Here you want to have a good timing so that you can work toward it. Failure to do this will be a very grave mistake because that you will not have the parameters to look into.

- Set priorities. Chances are that you have more than one goal. In this angle, you should always set the priorities of the goals that you want to achieve in life. You should arrange them based on their priority too.
- Write the goals down on paper. When you are creating goals, it is very important for you to write them down on paper, not on your computer. Write them on a piece of paper and then stick it somewhere so that you will see it every day. If you have a home office or desk, tape the paper to the desk so that, every time you sign into your email account, you will see it.
- Keep operational goals small. The next thing that you want to do with your goals is to keep the operational goals small. You basically don't want to work on very many things at the same time. Remember that you also want to enjoy life. When you start trying to achieve too many goals at the same time, it will make you lose focus.
- Always rely on performance goals. When setting goals, you could decide to set up performance goals or outcome goals. It is recommended that you set up performance goals. Doing this will be very significant for you. You want to set up goals that you totally control. When you are not in control, it will give you a lot of challenges at the end of the day. This is because you don't know what the other guys really want. You might not be able to achieve your goal within the given time frame, because you are relying on someone else to make your dream come true. But, if you focus on performance goals instead, you are only relying on yourself.
- Be as realistic as possible. This is where many people go wrong. Since they have heard that it is important to set goals, they go overboard and set goals that they can't even realize. For instance, imagine a situation where you want to be a billionaire in the next two weeks. How on earth will this goal be achieved? Where will all this money come from? Therefore, you should be very realistic at the end of the day. You should always have a sense that this is the real world as

you work toward these goals. You cannot set a goal that you want to fly a plane when you have not yet taken a lesson.

Achieving Goals

So what do you do when you finally achieve your life goal? How do you move on in all this? When you have achieved a goal, it is very important to enjoy all that it comes with. You should not be hard on yourself, and should instead make sure to give yourself a pat on the back for the hard work.

After you have done that, you should not rest very much. You should take time to reward yourself but keep remembering that the journey is not over. It is very important to review your goals, which will give you an edge on achieving the rest.

- If you have accomplished a goal easily, challenge yourself by setting a slightly more challenging goal.
- If, on the other hand, the goal took many years to be accomplished, you should now reduce the timeline for the next goal.
- It is also important to change the goals in the course of all this. If you learn something that is significant, then you should do the best to change and align it well.
- If you believe that you don't have the skills necessary for all of these, you should also learn these skills.

At times, you will fail to achieve your goals. This is absolutely normal, so don't be too hard on yourself or give up because of one failure. If you decide to take it positively, then you will ultimately achieve your goals. On the other hand, if you take it negatively, it will demoralize you and you will end up by quitting. You should take it as a lesson that will help you build the next stage of goals. You should also take it as a learning process. Remember that you can learn from failure the same as you learn from success.

Example of Goal Setting

As an example, this illustration will present a couple of key details about how a goal is set and accomplished.

As the year turns, a young lady by the name of Lenah decides to create goals that she wants to achieve in life.

The following are a couple of things that she decides to do:

1. Career—"To become the managing director of the company I work for."
2. Artistic—"I want to become a better artist with the aim of creating my own gallery where people can come and enjoy pieces of art. "
3. Physical—"I want to be good at athletics."

After setting the goals that she wants to accomplish later in life, Lenah decides that it is now time to break these goals into smaller tasks so that they can be manageable.

In the next part, the key details of what she wants to achieve in the short term have been highlighted. These are very important for her, as they will give her the motivation to work on a daily basis. She understands that she cannot open a gallery without taking care of a couple of preliminary details. This will focus on the career goal of becoming a managing director:

1. Five-year goal: "I want to become the deputy director."
2. Two-year goal: "I want to take relevant training toward an MBA, which will give me better chances."
3. One-year goal: "I will do some volunteer work for the organization together with the current managing director."
4. Six-month goal: "I want to liaise with the current director (who is retiring) to seek the relevant advice for his job."
5. One-week goal: "I will write a detailed letter of application explaining myself."

What this example clearly shows is that a big goal has been broken down into smaller goals that can be achieved without a lot of stress. Accomplishing the smaller goals is not all that hard when they are broken down into manageable segments.

What you should know about goal setting is that:

- It will help you to decide what you want to achieve in life.
- It will help you separate the relevant things from those that are irrelevant.
- They will also help you to motivate yourself.
- They should build your self-confidence.

In addition, it is important to set the lifetime goals first and foremost. After you have done this, you should now break them down into smaller goals that will help you achieve the goal that you have set. It is important not to lose focus in all this. As such, it is very important for you to keep reviewing your goals so that you can see whether you are on your way to achieving them or not.

If you don't have any goals in life, then start setting them right now. Chances are that when you use this goal-setting technique, you will have taken an important step toward achieving your goals.

Top Reasons Why Goals Fail

There are a number of key reasons why many people's goals fail. We will attempt to solve a couple of these issues in this part.

1. Limiting beliefs

The first main reason why many people's goals are never realized is that their belief system is usually affected. This is the process where they start having the so-called "wavering faith." This is the process where they start doubting whether they have the ability to achieve them. In many cases, it is a friend or relative who tells them that the goals are unachievable. The thing is that it is not good to believe what people have to say about you. They are not in your shoes. They are looking from the outside and they have no idea what you are truly capable of achieving. Only you can know that. Therefore, it is also important to believe in yourself no matter what people are saying about the goal that you have. Just as Henry Ford once said, you are always right when you think that you can or you can't. You should never doubt the inbuilt potential that you have in you all the time.

2. Creating the wrong goal

Another major reason why many people fail in accomplishing their goals, dreams, and aspirations is that they simply set the wrong goals. As stated above, goals should have the characteristic of being SMART. When you go ahead and set goals that are not SMART at all, then it is highly likely that you won't achieve these goals. There are a number of things that make goals that are hard to accomplish:

- When you set a goal just because someone else has set it. For instance, when you decide to do engineering just because all your friends are doing it.
- When you set a goal just to make other people happy.
- When you set a goal that you don't really love or care about. For instance, setting a goal as an engineer while your love is law.

Of course, these are mere examples. There are many other details that you should always think about when it comes to making your goals prosper. To see whether you are on the right path, you should take a pencil and a piece of paper and come up with the things that you want to achieve and write them a couple of times. The goal that keeps on coming back is the right goal for you.

3. Lack of consistency and patience

One thing that you should always know about goals is that they are not always very easy to accomplish. It takes people many years to accomplish the things that they have now. It took many years for Steve Jobs to create Apple and Bill Gates to create Microsoft.

4. Lack of action

At the beginning of the year, people come up with different resolutions of what they want to achieve later in life. Sadly, only a few people who set up these resolutions end up achieving the goals. This is simply because they don't work toward achieving the dreams and goals. If you know that you won't accomplish the goals that you set, then you should not even bother setting them at all.

Things to Remember

- Cognitive therapists have explored different ways to help people consider more constructive ways of thinking so that they can change the way they feel and respond to situations.
- Aaron Beck's cognitive therapy seeks to combine reversing the self-defeating thoughts with behavioral changes that formed what we know today as cognitive behavioral therapy. This therapy focuses on altering the way people act and think.
- CBT treatment begins with an assessment that allows the therapist to get a clear understanding of the issues that the client is suffering from, their current situation, and the changes they want to make.

- By setting goals, you are actually choosing where you want to go. By having a good picture of where you are going, chances are that you will be able to achieve your ambitions in life. With a goal, you will also be able to figure out the basic ways of avoiding the major distractions that could stand in your way.
- You should be very careful not to give up on the path of achieving your dreams. Every day wasted will end up pushing the goals further away from you until you don't even remember them.
- Always state the goal in a positive manner and be as realistic as possible.
- You should take time to reward yourself, but keep remembering that the journey is not over. It is very important to review your goals, which will give you an edge into achieving the rest.
- If you don't have any goals in life, you should do the right thing and start setting them right now. Chances are that, when you use this goal-setting technique, you will be on your way to achieving all your goals.
- To see whether you are on the right path, you should take a pencil and a piece of paper and come up with the things that you want to achieve and write them down a couple of times. The goal that keeps on coming back is the right goal for you.
- One thing that you should always know about goals is that they are not always very easy to accomplish. It takes people many years to accomplish the things that they have now.

Chapter Six: Cognitive Techniques

As a person, you are bombarded with thousands of thoughts every day. These thoughts influence how you feel and respond to situations. As human beings, we tend to assume that our thoughts accurately reflect reality, that our thoughts are facts. However, in CBT we are asking you to stand back and identify those thoughts that are associated with the negative emotions you would like to work on addressing. To start to view these thoughts as opinions rather than facts, opinions that may or may not be true. In this section, we will review some strategies for how to identify and challenge the thoughts and underlying beliefs that are connected to your distress.

Automatic Thoughts

Automatic thoughts are thoughts that pop into your mind without any conscious control. When someone experiences an unhealthy negative emotion, we say that the person may have been experiencing a *negative automatic thought.*

Thinking Errors

Below is a list of common patterns of thinking that often go along with unhealthy negative emotions.

All-Or-Nothing Thinking

When you see things in black and white categories, such as success or failure.

"I made a mistake. I'm such a failure."

Mind Reading

You think people are having negative thoughts about you without checking this out.

"She thinks I'm boring."

Emotional Reasoning

Assuming that your emotions reflect reality: "I feel it so it must be true."

"I feel stupid so I must really be stupid."

I Can't Stand It

You have a low frustration tolerance. You think the situation is so bad that it is intolerable.

"This is intolerable."

"Should" Statements

You use "should" or "must" statements to apply rules to your own or other people's behavior.

"I should always be in control."
"Other people should work as hard as I do."

Fortune-Telling Error

You predict the future and anticipate that things are going to turn out badly.

"My boss asked me to see him later today, so I must be in trouble."

Labeling

You attach a global negative label to yourself or other people.

"I'm just a loser."
"He is stupid."

Discounting the Positive

You dismiss positive experiences by saying that they don't count.

For example, a person compliments on your appearance, but you decide that person is just being nice.

An advantage of identifying which thinking errors you identify with is that it is a good first step toward allowing you to stand back from your thoughts and question them. You can start to capture your thoughts and say, "There is another one of those fortune-telling thoughts."

Situation	**A person has just submitted a report to their boss and now their boss wants to see them.**
Thoughts/Cognition	**Oh no! I did a really bad job and I am in trouble with the boss.**

Physical Feelings/Psychological effects	**Feeling sick, sweating.**
Emotional Feelings	**Anxious**
Behaviors	**Walks into the boss's office apologizing for report.**
Thinking error	**Fortune telling**

The aim of CBT is to help clients recognize the negative automatic thoughts they are experiencing and consider more balanced, helpful alternatives.

Have a go at practicing using the thought record below any time you are experiencing an unhealthy negative emotion.

THOUGHT RECORD EXAMPLE

Step 1: Situation/adversity

I was in my dental surgery treating a patient. The patient became upset and stated that he was going to make a formal complaint against me.

Step 2: Automatic Thought(s)

"This idiot shouldn't be talking to me like this."

Step 3: Emotion

Angry

Step 4: Balanced alternative response

a) What evidence do I have that this automatic thought is true?

I don't have any evidence to suggest that patients shouldn't be rude (I would just prefer that they weren't).

b) What evidence do I have that does not support this thought?

The only evidence I have is that he did talk to me like that.

c) If someone I really cared about had gone through this situation and had the same automatic thoughts and feelings, what would I say to them that would be helpful?

If my colleague Hilary had gone through this situation I would tell her that it's certainly not nice to be talked to in a negative way by patients, but some people get anxious and overreact when at the dentist.

d) Is this a helpful thought to have? If not, why not? Would I teach a class of 5-year-olds to think this way?

This thought is not helpful because it makes me feel angrier and that doesn't help me calm the patient down. I wouldn't teach a class of 5-year-olds to conclude that other people are idiots when they don't talk to you in the way you would like them to.

e) Does this thought make logical sense?

It doesn't really make logical sense to say that because I would like the patient not to talk to me in this way that they necessarily should behave the way I want them to.

f) Does this thought fit in with any of the thinking errors?

The thought fits with one of those "should" statements. Also, I'm "labeling" the patient in a negative way.

g) What is the worst that could happen? What is the best that could happen? What is the most realistic outcome?

The absolute worst that could happen is that I get struck off from the dental register for professional malpractice. The best that could happen is that I have a conversation with the patient and he calms down and decides against making a complaint. The most likely outcome is that the patient remains somewhat angry but the complaint gets sorted out without it going further and causing problems with my professional registration.

New perspective: I would really prefer he didn't talk to me like this but there is no reason he mustn't. He is not acting in the best way right now but that doesn't mean he's an idiot.

Step 5: Outcome

I would validate how the patient is feeling and offer to talk over his concerns in a non-defensive manner and negotiate a fair way of resolving the dispute.

Thought Record

Step 1: Situation/adversity

When you notice your mood getting worse, write down what was happening just before you started to feel this way. What situation are you in and what event just took place? Did you notice a distressing physical sensation? Did you notice experiencing a series of negative thoughts? What was the most difficult part of this situation?

Step 2: Automatic Thought(s)

What thoughts or images went through your mind?

Step 3: Emotion

What emotion did you experience (depression, anxiety, guilt, hurt, shame, jealousy, envy, etc.)?

Step 4: Balanced alternative response

Now ask yourself the following questions to help develop a more helpful perspective. Write down this new more balanced perspective.

a) What evidence do I have that this automatic thought is true?
b) What evidence do I have that does not support this thought?
c) If someone I really cared about had gone through this situation and had the same automatic thoughts and feelings, what would I say to them that would be helpful?
d) Is this a helpful thought to have? If not, why not? Would I teach a class of 5-year-old children to think this way?
e) Does this thought make logical sense?
f) Does this thought fit in with any of the thinking errors?
g) What is the worst that could happen? What is the best that could happen? What is the most realistic outcome?

Now summarize the above into a new helpful perspective to answer back your original negative automatic thought.

Step 5: Outcome

Now that you have written down an alternative, more balanced thought, ask yourself to imagine for a moment that you believed this viewpoint 100%. If you believed it 100%, what new behaviors could you practice engaging in the next time this issue presents itself in your life? Write these new behaviors down.

How to Deal with Negative Thoughts

The fact is that everyone has negative thoughts once in a while. The biggest challenge is how they handle these thoughts. When you are sick, you can come up with a statement like, "Even though this is a major challenge right now because I have a lot of work to do this week, I believe that after a few days, I will get better and be back at work." This is a better statement than when you say something like, "I feel terrible, this could not have come at a worse time, and I will never get over it." The latter appreciates that there is a problem and prophesies a negative outcome while the former sees a light at the end of the tunnel.

Just take a moment to carry out this exercise. Go outside and sit down in an open place. Don't take anything, including your phone. Once you are there, start thinking of anything that you have in mind. Do you have something negative that you are thinking about? Remember that you are the master of your mind. It can be helpful to start to label your thoughts, so rather than thinking "I'm a failure," tell yourself, "I'm having a thought…that I am a failure." This can help you start to view your thoughts as just that: thoughts rather than reality. You can try this with any troubling thoughts you are having. Just put "I'm having a thought" before your automatic thought. Don't allow your thoughts to bully you or to push you around.

Tips to be Happier and More Positive in Life

Now we will look at a couple of things that you could do to become happier in life. When these things are done, chances are that you will be putting yourself in a good position to make the most of life.

- Be yourself and live for the moment; this means that you should focus on where you are today and not where you will be tomorrow. If you have some issues, then tell yourself that this is just a passing cloud. The sun is always shining above the clouds.
- Be open to people around you. The thing is that, when you share problems with someone who is really close to you, you will be good to go.
- Also, you can decide to treat yourself. For instance, you can decide to play with your kids one afternoon or go shopping.
- Eat well: Just because you have some issues is not an excuse for you to starve yourself or binge on unhealthy food. You should eat a nicely cooked meal. It is amazing what wonders this can do for you.

The ABC's of Beliefs

The famous psychologist Albert Ellis was one of the original founders of the cognitive behavioral therapy approach, along with Aaron Beck. Ellis utilized the ABC framework to help clients and therapists understand how our beliefs contribute to our emotional and behavioral responses to events.

A = Activating event/adversity

B = Belief

C = Consequences (emotion and behavior)

As human beings, we often think that events cause our feelings. You hear people say, "My boss made me angry when he criticized my presentation." The ABC framework questions this perspective by saying that something comes between things that happen to us in life (the A) and our emotional response (the C) and that is our beliefs (the B). There can be a variety of ways of thinking about being criticized by your boss; some of these ways lead to healthy negative emotions and some lead to unhealthy negative emotions.

Ellis proposed that our unhealthy negative emotions can be explained by our tendency to hold rigid, inflexible beliefs about ourselves, other people, or the world. These beliefs are often in the form of a SHOULD or MUST. So the person might be holding the belief, *My boss should not have criticized my presentation and I can't stand that he did.* It is this belief that causes the unhealthy anger. Ellis therefore proposed that if clients could identify the beliefs that they are holding that drive their unhealthy negative emotions and replace these with more flexible ones, they could change how they feel when confronted with adversities in their lives.

Ellis put forward the idea that the more flexible alternative beliefs often involve holding a strong preference rather than a demand; so an alternative preferential belief could be stated in the format of, *I would really like it if my boss did not criticize my presentation but there is no rule that he absolutely mustn't. It is difficult to stand being criticized, but I can stand it.*

The problem ABC:

A – Adversity – My boss criticizing my presentation.

B – Belief – *My boss absolutely should not have criticized my presentation. I can't stand that he criticized it.*

C – Consequences

Emotion – Unhealthy Anger

Behavior – Make a sarcastic comment to my boss.

The alternative ABC:

A – Adversity – My boss criticizing my presentation.

B – Belief – *I would really like it if my boss did not criticize my presentation but there is no rule that he absolutely must not. It is difficult to stand being criticized, but I can stand it.*

C – Consequences –

Emotion – Healthy Anger

Behavior – Listen carefully to the feedback from my boss.

Components of health and unhealthy beliefs	
Unhealthy beliefs	Healthy beliefs
You hold a rigid *demand* in the form of a should or a must; e.g., I must get an A on my exam.	You hold a flexible *preference* such as: "I would really like to" but you don't turn this preference into a demand. So, for example, "I would really like to get an A on my exam but there is no reason I absolutely must get an A."
You hold a *low frustration tolerance* belief in the form of "I can't stand it." So, for example: I couldn't stand it if I didn't get an A on my exam.	You hold a *high frustration tolerance* belief in the form of "It would be difficult to cope with but I would cope with it." So, for example: "It would certainly be very difficult to cope with not getting an A but I could

	stand the discomfort of not achieving this grade."
You hold an *awfulizing* belief. You tell yourself that it's awful when things don't go your way. So, for example: "It's awful that I didn't get the grade I was aiming to achieve."	You hold an *anti-awfulizing* belief by telling yourself that nothing in life, however bad, is in fact awful. So, for example: "It's really bad and unfortunate that I didn't achieve an A on the exam but it's in no way awful."
You put yourself or others down by holding a *self and/or other-downing* belief. So, for example: "I am just a stupid idiot for not doing as well as I wanted in the exam. My professor is such an idiot for not teaching us well."	You hold a *self-acceptance* and *other-acceptance* belief. So, for example: "The fact I didn't do as well as I would have liked in my exam shows that I am a fallible human being just like everyone else."

So you can use the ABC format to help yourself change your feelings and behaviors by identifying and questioning your beliefs. You can do this any time that you experience an unhealthy negative emotion in one of the situations in your life that you have identified as one you would like to work on.

One way of working out the emotion you are experiencing is by looking at your behavior or how you feel like behaving (Dryden, 2009). Unhealthy negative emotions lead people to behave in self-defeating ways. Healthy negative emotions lead people to behave in a way that is helpful to them.

Emotion	Theme of emotion	Behaviors
Anxiety	Threat	Avoid the threat.

		Escape from the threat. Take precautions in an attempt to reduce the threat.
Depression	Loss	Avoid doing things. Procrastinate. Ruminate on negative thoughts. Withdraw from life situations.
Hurt	Being treated badly by others	Stop talking to the other person.
Guilt	Having done something wrong	Punish self. Beg for forgiveness.
Shame	Shameful information has been revealed	Hide self away from others.
Envy	Someone possesses something desirable that you don't have	Say that the possession is of little worth. Take the possession from the other person.
Jealousy	Threat perceived to personal relationship	Check up on the fidelity of partner. Regularly seek reassurance from partner.
Anger	A personal rule has been broken	Attack self or other physically or verbally.

Use the framework below to monitor your ABC's in your problem situations.

A – Adversity/situation

Ask yourself what happened just before you started to experience the emotion or behavior at C.

B – Beliefs

Ask yourself, "What was I telling myself about this adversity?

What am I demanding about myself, other people or the world?"

e.g., I must … (not make mistakes)/other people must … (respect me)/the world must … (give me what I want)

Are you holding a low frustration tolerance belief?

Are you holding an awfulizing belief?

Are you holding a self-downing belief or an other-downing belief?

C – Consequences

Emotion—What emotion did I experience?

Behavior—What did I do in terms of my behavior?

Once you have had a go at monitoring your ABC, you can ask yourself a series of the disputing questions to help you identify a more helpful alternative belief.

D – Disputing

Is this a helpful belief? Why or why not?

Does this belief make logical sense?

What evidence do I have that supports this belief?

What about evidence that doesn't support this belief?

Is this belief flexible or rigid?

E – New effective response

What new belief or rule would you like to adopt that may get you a better outcome in future situations?

e.g., I would prefer … (to be liked by all my colleague *but* I don't have to be; it's bad to be disliked, but not awful).

Is your new belief helpful?

Does your new belief make sense?

Would you be happy to teach this belief to a class of 5-year-old children?

You basically have modified your irrational DEMAND to a logical PREFERENCE.

Your new belief will help you experience a healthy negative emotion (e.g., concern rather than severe anxiety). This less extreme emotion will help you to practice behaving in a way that gets you a better outcome.

How Life Experiences Lead to the Development of Beliefs

In order to really understand the development of unhelpful beliefs, you need to consider the connection between your (negative) life experiences and the development of your core beliefs about yourself (e.g., I am inadequate) and core beliefs about others (e.g., other people are untrustworthy) and the world (e.g., it's dog eat dog).

As human beings, how we interpret day-to-day situations can be influenced by the kind of experiences that we have had in life. These life experiences influence the beliefs we hold, which in turn influence how we view daily situations. If we have lots of experiences in life of being criticized by others, we might understandably pick up a belief that other people are generally critical. Daily situations are more likely to be interpreted through this belief system, which serves as a biased filter. Any information that fits the idea of others being critical is easily noticed. Information that doesn't support this viewpoint is either not noticed or is discounted. In this way, other people's neutral behavior will be interpreted as having a critical motive.

Feelings such as anxiety, depression, anger, and guilt are often rooted in low opinions of oneself in the form of unhelpful beliefs. If you regularly battle with negative thoughts about yourself, you might very well suffer from problems with low self-esteem. If you believe that you are only worthwhile if you are achieving highly in the office, in finance, or in attractiveness, your self-esteem will plummet the minute those parts of your life are not going well. Self-esteem is rooted in the idea of estimating or measuring your worth. If you are faced with low self-esteem, then you believe yourself to be estimated or measured as low in value, and vice versa.

Consider Heather again…

Heather grew up with a mother and a father until she was a young teen, when her father left. That being said, her mother was overprotective of her early on to shield her from any further heartache as she grew up.

Her life experience was, therefore, being overprotected by her mother growing up.

This overprotectiveness made Heather develop the core belief that she was incompetent and could not do anything on her own, or at least not without someone else like her mother or a husband.

Her assumption is that, if she relies on someone else, then she is strong, capable, and can cope with her life.

But, with that said, her current problem is that she cannot take on new projects without excessive reassurance from her husband, constantly telling her that she is worth something and can accomplish things with his support.

Understanding Heather in the context of her difficulties:

(Negative) Life Experiences

Dad left when I was entering teenage years.

Mum was highly protective of me.

Core Beliefs

I am incompetent.

Other people are strong and capable.

Assumptions/Rules for Living

If I can rely on others, then I can cope.

I must not make any mistakes.

Trigger situations (situations where rules for living may be broken)

Being asked to take on new projects at work.

Automatic thoughts: I won't do it properly.

Emotion: Anxiety

Behavior: Ask colleague for reassurance

And what about Michael?

Michael's father worked full time at the local steel mill, leaving his mother in control of the home. Both exhausted with their lives, Michael's father was typically found at the local bar while his mother quietly read scriptures at the kitchen table. His father once told Michael that he should never complain because this was all to be expected out of life and having a significant other was all that mattered, but being ungrateful and complaining might drive them away. Father constantly criticized Michael. Neither parent talked much about their feelings nor did they give Michael much encouragement throughout his childhood. The only perceived model available for a comfortable lifestyle was to follow in the same footsteps.

This made Michael succumb to an unhappy lifestyle and never voice his personal feelings for fear of being rejected or losing his spouse.

The assumption Michael has is that he should never voice his complaints and should only accept his unhappy life with his wife because he is nothing without her. That said, his current problem is that he cannot express his true dissatisfaction with his marriage or his fears about his career steps.

Understanding Michael in the context of his difficulties:

<u>(Negative) Life Experiences</u>

Parent never discussed problems or feelings and placed a lot of importance on marriage.

Never received any encouragement from parents and dad was highly critical.

<u>Core Beliefs</u>

I am worthless.

Other people are critical.

<u>Assumptions/Rules for living</u>

If I talk about my feelings, then I will be rejected.

If I can maintain the perfect marriage, then I am worthwhile.

If I show signs of anxiety, then people will humiliate me.

<u>Trigger situations (situations where rules for living may be broken)</u>

Marital disagreements, Job interviews

Automatic thoughts: She is upset with me.

Emotion: Anxious

Behavior: Try to keep wife happy.

It is important to understand that every human has extrinsic value to other people and intrinsic value to themselves. We, as humans, typically confuse these two classifications and try instead to base our intrinsic value on what other people feel about us. Humans change regularly, are dynamic creatures, complex and fallible. This is what makes humans so unique. And yet people often define their entire worth on the basis of individual components, judging self-worth based on a few "bad" things. But consider that a bowl of freshly picked fruit is bound to have some pieces that are bruised or have been scavenged by insects, yet you would not consider the entire bowl to be worthless. This same viewpoint ought to be applied to ourselves.

That being said, it is important that you avoid labeling yourself based on single events or emotions. If you lied to your mother once, that does not make you a liar forever. If you smoked cigarettes for two months in your 20s, that does not make you a smoker forever. If you failed a project once over the course of your career, you are not a failure forever. And, by the same token, if you achieved success in one task, that does not make you successful forever. It is for this reason that you must avoid basing your self-esteem on a single experience, action, or incident.

You are based on the totality of your characteristics, not on a single one, a single thought, or a single intention. As such, finding the life experiences that stand at the root of your core beliefs about yourself can help you to rectify those beliefs.

If you find out that your core beliefs that people are untrustworthy is based on a single life experience wherein a close friend betrayed your trust, then you can learn to let go of that event, learn to forgive the flaws in other people and yourself until you reach a point where they no longer result in unhealthy thoughts and behaviors you hold about everyone.

Many people overlook imperfections they have while condemning those same imperfections in other people. This relates directly to what you believe to be important, your level of self-esteem, and your flexibility. For example, you might be a good student, but you struggle with examinations and, in spite of earnest studying, you often forget what you learned come test day.

With that in mind, you need to recognize that you cannot change everything about who you are. Sometimes you can improve upon those things, but other times there is no way to change it. The key is recognizing where you can make a change and where you cannot. Living a rewarding life means accepting your limitations, avoiding putting yourself down because of these limitations, and capitalizing on the strengths that you have. Given the example above, you can review your current study habits to see if there are ways in which you might study more effectively. Or you might recognize that this is one of those things that cannot be changed, and you will simply be a person who does better with practical work tasks than with written examinations. If you choose to accept yourself for who you are and work on those areas where you can improve, you will learn to embrace the fallibility that is being human.

This applies not just to yourself, but to others. Learning from these personal habits will eventually lead to a better understanding of those around you, too. You might know that your friend has a poor memory and can often remember the events, but not the people who were in them. By recognizing that they are fallible like yourself, and that they work hard to improve upon limitations that can be improved upon, you will recognize that this type of memory-related issue is not something they can change and you will, therefore, learn to forgive that person for forgetting that you were with them when they met that famous movie star or saw that adorable puppy. This will allow you to forgive them, accept them for who they are, and avoid taking it personally that they did not remember you were with them.

How to Identify Your Unhelpful Beliefs Using the Downward Arrow Technique

It is important to identify unhelpful beliefs and assumptions that you may have. The downward arrow technique functions as a tool that enables you to uncover your belief systems influencing behavior and emotions. In most cases, people are unclear as to the beliefs that influence their mood and actions, and learning what they are makes it easier to avoid acting upon them and giving into patterns of self-defeating thinking.

In order to find out a core belief, you should:

1) Write down a thought that popped into your head during a recent distressing situation where you experienced an unhealthy negative emotion.

2) Temporarily assume that this thought is true and then ask yourself what that thought means to you or about you.

3) Keep repeating this until you find your underlying core belief.

Michael and his therapist had a go at using the downward arrow technique following a situation where Michael felt anxious when his wife frowned at him during a conversation over dinner. He identified one of the automatic thoughts that popped into his head was "She is fed up with me."

Michael: "She is fed up with me."

Therapist: Michael if you temporarily assumed that this thought is true, what does it mean to you?

Michael: She is unhappy with our relationship.

Therapist: And if it were true that she is unhappy with your relationship, what would that mean to you?

Michael: Sooner or later she will find someone else.

Therapist: And if that did happen, what would that mean to you?

Michael: It would mean that I have messed up the only important thing in my life.

Therapist: And if you had messed up the only important thing in your life, what would that say about you?

Michael: That I am worthless.

Therapist: So, Michael, it sounds like you are saying that you are only worthwhile if everything is going perfectly in your relationship, is that right? If so, this may be one of your unhelpful assumptions. Also, it sounds like underlying this you are holding more of a fundamental belief about yourself that you are worthless. Have I got that right?

Michael: Yes, I think that does sound correct because I feel worthless in lots of situations generally in my life. I have always felt worthless.

Now see if you can have a go at using the downward arrow technique to uncover your core belief.

Identify a recent specific situation where you felt distressed. Identify one of the automatic thoughts that popped into your mind at the time.

Automatic thought: ....

And if you assumed that thought is true, what would that mean to you?

…………………………………………………………..

What would that mean to you or about you?

…………………………………………………………..

Now that you have identified some of your beliefs, you can start to add them to your own individual understanding of your difficulties below. At the top, write down any significant life experiences that stand out as important in forming how you have learned to think about yourself and others. Underneath make a note of your core beliefs, assumptions (if…then..) and rules for living (I must…). Finally, write down situations in your life that cause you a problem and activate you underlying beliefs. Write down the most typical automatic thoughts, feelings, and behaviors that come up for you in these situations.

(Negative) Life Experiences

↓

Core Beliefs

I am…

Other people are…

↓

Assumptions/Rules for living

If……………then……….

I must…………

Other people must…………

↓

Trigger situations (situations where rules for living may be broken)

Situation:

Automatic thoughts:

Emotion:

Behavior:

How to Challenge Core Beliefs

In some cases, you may recognize that your core belief is untrue. But, in other cases, people really do have a strong level of belief in their core beliefs. If you would like to work on challenging your core beliefs and developing new, helpful ways of thinking about yourself, then you can start by making a list of experiences that you have had in your life that show that your core belief is not true all of the time. Heather decided to challenge her belief that she is incompetent.

Heather's old core belief: I am incompetent.

Heather's new alternative core belief: I am a person with both strengths and weaknesses.

Heather created a list of experiences that didn't support her old core belief:

- I beat other applicants at interview to be offered my current job.
- I'm organized and manage to plan our weekly food shopping.
- I returned a damaged item of clothing to the shop and negotiated a refund.
- I graduated from college.
- I play a musical instrument at a relatively high level.
- I managed to learn enough French to get by on our holiday to Paris.

Have a go at trying this process yourself.

Write down your old core belief:

Write down your new, more helpful core belief:

Create a list of experiences that don't support your old core belief:

-
-
-
-
-
-

Acting as if your new core belief is 100% true is a further way of increasing how strongly you connect intellectually and emotionally with this new belief. Heather decided to act as if she was a person who is competent and had strengths in a number of areas. She identified the fact that this would fit in with her doing more things independently without asking others for reassurance. She consistently behaved in ways that logically fit with her new belief and found that, with consistent practice over time, her new belief started to feel truer for her.

You may also benefit from going through this process of *acting as if* your new core belief were 100% true. Imagine you are being paid as an actor who believes your new belief 100%. How would you be approaching daily situations differently? What would you be doing more of in terms of your behavior? What would you be doing less of in terms of your behavior? Pick one of two behaviors to specifically practice in the coming week. Continue to behave in ways that support your new health core belief. With consistent practice over time, this is likely to make you think and feel differently about yourself. A further way of testing your beliefs is by setting up behavioral experiments.

How to Test New Alternative Helpful Beliefs by Carrying Out Behavioral Experiments

Challenging your thinking using the thought diary is often helpful. However, it can be even more powerful to practice acting on new ways of thinking by carrying out behavioral experiments. Behavioral experiments are like science experiments, but in CBT we help people change their behavior to test their beliefs. Behavioral experiments can be used to test out the accuracy of your beliefs and test new perspectives. The key here is that you can often undermine problems like anxiety by identifying the beliefs that drive the emotion and then test the accuracy of these by setting up an experiment.

Discovery Experiments

Discovery experiments are done when you want to learn what would happen if you were to act in a different way. An example is John, who works in a bank. John holds the belief that none of his colleagues like him and therefore he must be unlikable as a person. As a result of holding this belief, John tends to keep to himself when at work and does not engage in any small talk with his colleagues. John may stand back and start to question his belief that he is unlikable. Maybe he develops a new belief that he is generally a likable person. He could test out this alternative belief by behaving differently at work with his colleagues. He could identify one or two behaviors to work on during the week. Perhaps he starts by experimenting with smiling and saying good morning to his colleagues. Or joining his colleagues for a coffee at break and asking them some questions about their weekend. These new behaviors for John could help him start to get experimental with his beliefs and collect some new evidence that may help update his beliefs. John may well feel anxious before giving this a go and might be quite unsure about the outcome beforehand.

Observational Experiments

Observational experiments are those in which you play the role of the observer. Your purpose is to test for discovery or even to test a hypothesis that you have. Direct observation is where you might, for example, monitor the way you or other people react to a situation that brings about anxiety for you. With the new information about how you or others act, you can learn ways to change your behavior.

For example, let's imagine that you feel anxious about talking to your partner about particular topics, such as your sex life. As a result, you avoid discussing this with your partner. When you stand back and consider what belief you are holding that seems to drive your anxiety, you realize that you hold a belief about yourself as being weak and unable to managing difficult conversations. You predict that your partner will get irritated and walk out of the room if you raise the topic for discussion and you won't cope with this. You could test this out by confronting this normally avoided situation and observing your own behavior and that of your partner. This could allow you an opportunity to test the accuracy of your hypothesis and beliefs.

Sometimes people may learn that some of their behaviors in situations like this might actually unintentionally reinforce their negative beliefs. In this case, you may learn from your observation that you start talking in an indirect passive way with you partner about this issue, resulting in you not getting it resolved. This may lead to a reflection that your indirect style of communicating reinforces the idea you are weak. You need to practice communicating more directly with people.

In addition to the thoughts about internal events and external situations, you may have some situation-specific negative automatic thoughts that you can target through experiments. Let's imagine you have the thought that people will think you are boring if you have a conversation with them. You predict that if that thought were true, you would notice that the person you are talking with would look away from you or frown. You experiment with talking to two new people a day and watch their reactions closely to help you collect some evidence to test this thought.

Learning from Behavioral Experiments

Learning from behavioral experiments means preparing the experiment, experiencing the situation, making observations, and reflecting upon the results of your behavioral experiment. It is important that you consider your own feelings, your thoughts, and your behavior during any experiment. The observations made should be reflected upon in order to make the most of this experience.

Consider Michael again:

Michael has set himself a goal of being able to make positive requests to his wife about activities he would like to do with her. He is a 40-year-old man who is currently having marital difficulties. He finds his marriage unsatisfying because his wife doesn't spend much time with him during her free time. He struggles to express this dissatisfaction with his wife, as the thought of doing so leaves him anxious and worried that she will leave him.

Beliefs:

What thoughts/beliefs are you testing out? See if you can have a go at identifying if there could be alternative thoughts/beliefs that may be more accurate or helpful for you to hold.

Current belief: If I express my wishes to others then they will reject me (I believe this 80%).

____

______________________________Alternative belief: It's okay to express my wishes and opinions (I currently believe this 10%)

Experiment:

Good experiments often involve confronting avoided situations or having a go at behaving in a new way. Which are you trying out?

I will try confronting a situation that I normally avoid, which would be to make a positive request to my wife to go out for a meal in the new restaurant in town.

Prediction:

What do you predict will happen?

I think my wife may be unhappy with the suggestion and not want to go.

How will you know if your prediction was right?

She will tell me she doesn't want to go out for dinner.

Outcome:

What happened?

I did feel quite anxious having a go at discussing this with my wife but, in the end, she did say she would be happy to try the new restaurant. She didn't seem unhappy or upset.

Was the outcome what you expected?

It seemed to go a bit better than expected.

Learning:

What did you learn? What might be a good follow-up experiment?

I learned that perhaps it's okay for me to express my wishes or opinions to others and it is unlikely to lead to my being rejected.

Follow-up experiments could be expressing my wishes more often with other people more generally rather than just always doing what other people want to do.

Consider Heather again:

Heather decided to set up an experiment to test her belief that she is incompetent.

Beliefs:

What thoughts/beliefs are you testing out? See if you can have a go at identifying if there could be alternative thoughts/beliefs that may be more accurate or helpful for you to hold.

Current belief: I am incompetent (I believe this 70%).

____Alternative belief: I am a person with both strengths and weaknesses (I currently believe this 20%).

Experiment:

Good experiments often involve confronting avoided situations or having a go at behaving in a new way. Which are you trying out?

I will try calling the hospital to find out how long I will have to wait for an appointment with the consultant regarding my operation.

Prediction:

What do you predict will happen?

I predict that I won't be able to express myself well enough to be understood and get an answer.

Outcome:

What happened?

The receptionist was rather abrupt, but I managed to get the information I was after despite this and she seemed to understand what I was saying.

Was the outcome what you expected?

No, I still managed to be understood and get the information I was after.

Learning:

What did you learn? What might be a good follow-up experiment?

I learned that I can do things by myself such as making challenging phone calls. This shows that I do have strengths in some areas.

You can use the worksheet below to start practicing your own behavioral experiments.

Beliefs:

What thoughts/beliefs are you testing? See if you can identify whether there could be alternative thoughts/beliefs that may be more accurate or helpful for you to hold.

____

____

Experiment:

Good experiments often involve confronting avoided situations or having a go at behaving in a new way. Which are you trying out?

Prediction:

What do you predict will happen?

How will you know if your prediction was right?

Outcome:

What happened?

Was the outcome what you expected?

Learning:

What did you learn? What might be a good follow-up experiment?

It is important to understand that people will behave as though their assumptions, their thoughts, and their beliefs are valid. In this case, the behavior of each person makes sense based on what they believe is real, but this exact belief is what prevents some people from updating an older perspective. In anxiety disorders especially, it is important to identify what unhelpful behaviors, often safety-seeking behaviors, are used. This means discovering what you think will happen if you fail to engage in any precautions you use to prevent your fears coming true. For example, if a person holds the belief that they will collapse if they go into a busy shopping mall, then they may tend to take the precaution of always holding on to something. However, this precaution may unintentionally maintain their fear by preventing them from learning that they wouldn't collapse even if they didn't hold on to something. It can therefore be important to try dropping your precautions when doing experiments.

As you are conducting these experiments outside of the therapist's office, you will want to engage in independent experiments at home, in places where the experiment might best serve your desired outcome. For example, if you want to test how a certain thought pattern affects your daily functioning, you would need to conduct the observational experiment for a day or two across the main places you go, such as your home and your office, or the store and church. You want to observe in all of the situations in which you find yourself daily.

You also need to consider the people and the resources you will need. If you are recording your observations, you might want an audio recorder and video recorder, or if you are out and about for work or while you run errands, you might be able to best record your observations with a journal in which to write and a tape recorder on which to record thoughts when you cannot write them down. If you feel as though increasing your confidence in the experiment is only going to happen if someone else is with you, such as a partner or family member, then you must ask them to get involved with the experiment ahead of time.

When you are planning your experiments, you may encounter problems with real-life scenarios, especially when other people are involved in your experiment. You may not be able to eliminate all of the unexpected, but you can ask yourself what problems you think might arise and how you might handle them.

Your experiment may have an unanticipated outcome, but that is perfectly fine. With open-mindedness about your experiment and avoiding a "no lose" experience, you can still learn something from your experiment that might help you manage your negative automatic thoughts.

For example, if you hypothesize that most people are mean and rude, you might design an observational experiment whereby you would visit a shopping mall and observe people passing by you. You would take note of what you determined to be "mean" or "rude" behaviors versus "nice" and "polite" behaviors, such as smiling versus glaring, making eye contact versus avoiding eye contact, or stopping to talk versus yelling or ignoring. Then you would make note of the behaviors you observed most in your encounter. The results would be how many of each thing was observed and you would have to assess the outcome based on what the results showed. So, if your results indicated that 25 out of 27 people who walked by you smiled, made eye contact, or stopped to talk to you, then you would have to conclude that most people are nice and polite.

Things to Remember

- The fact is that everyone has negative thoughts once in a while. The biggest challenge now has to do with how they handle these thoughts.
- To really understand the development of unhelpful beliefs, you need to consider the connection between your (negative) life experiences and the development of your core beliefs about them self (e.g., I am inadequate) and core beliefs about others (e.g., other people are untrustworthy).
- The downward arrow technique functions as a tool that enables you to uncover the belief systems that influence your behavior and emotions.
- Behavioral experiments can help you to collect evidence to test out your beliefs and consider alternative theories.
- It is important that you consider your own feelings, your thoughts, your behavior, and your body sensations during any experiment. The observations made should be reflected upon to gain the most out of the experiment.

Chapter Seven: Behavioral Techniques

In addition to the cognitive techniques you are using, there are many behavioral techniques that can help you to reduce unhelpful behaviors and help you to take steps toward achieving your goals. These skills are incredibly important and they work in tandem with the cognitive skills already covered in this book.

Most people don't know much about the factors that affect how they behave daily. Without having this information, it's difficult for you to change your behavior. Research has demonstrated that several principles affect how people learn to behave in particular ways and how these behaviors are maintained over time.

What happens immediately after you engage in a behavior is important in determining the probability of your repeating this behavior. Some of your behaviors will be followed by consequences that increase the probably. When this happens, the behavior has been *reinforced.* When a behavior is followed by your getting something that you want, then we might say that this behavior has been *positively reinforced.* Human beings often want different things, so what reinforces a behavior for one person may not reinforce the same behavior for someone else. However, behaviors can often be reinforced when, immediately after the behavior, you get to engage in an activity or hobby you enjoy. Alternatively, your behavior may be reinforced when you get a response from people around you that you like. Some people may find gaining the attention of others or receiving praise as reinforcing. It's not that we are deliberately engaged in the behavior in question to get attention or praise but, if it immediately follows our behavior and we find these consequences desirable, then the behavior will be reinforced.

When our behavior is immediately followed by the removal of something that we don't want, then the behavior has been *negatively reinforced.* Engaging in a behavior that results in the removal of a negative emotion, negative thought, or uncomfortable physical sensation will tend to reinforce that behavior. So, for example, if you feel anxious about attending a job interview and you decide to call them up at the last minute to say you can't attend, you may feel less anxious because you don't have to face this challenging situation. In this way, calling up to cancel job interviews at the last minute may be negatively reinforced. So, when you are faced with job interviews again in the future, you are likely to call them and cancel at the last minute. Positive and negative reinforcement can serve to maintain your tendency to repeat particular behavior's over time.

When the consequences of a behavior decrease the probability of this behavior being repeated then it has been *punished.* Behaviors can be punished when they are followed by something unwanted. So, if I complimented my wife and she criticized me for complimenting her, then my behavior of complimenting her was punished. I would therefore be less likely to compliment her again in future as I dislike being criticized. Behaviors can also be punished when they are followed by something that you like being taken away. So if I complimented my wife and immediately she walked into the kitchen and then poured my favorite beer down the sink then this would understandable decrease the probability of my complimenting her again in future.

So you need to learn which of your behaviors are currently being followed by consequences that are reinforcing and punishing. In particular, you need to decide which behaviors you would like to work on reducing or increasing and then start to monitor times when you engage in this behavior in order to find what the consequences of this behavior are. If you are working on changing your behavior, you will need to decide what you will replace your old behavior with. What is your desired goal behavior? What specifically would we see you doing if we were watching a video of you performing your goal behavior? You could create a list like the one below.

Behaviors I would like to work on reducing:	*What my new goal behavior will be:*
1. Seeking reassurance from my wife	Instead of seeking reassurance, my goal is to sit and write down my worries onto a piece of paper.
2. Putting off addressing my problems	Instead, my goal is to have a 10-minute period each day after dinner when I will sit down and write down all my problems and do some problem solving.
3. Drinking too much alcohol	Instead my goal is to have a non-alcoholic drink whenever I am around alcohol.
4. Avoiding talking to people I don't know	Instead my goal is to go over and initiate a conversation with someone whom I have not spoken to before.

Now you have a go:

Behaviors I would like to work on reducing:	*What my new goal behavior will be:*

What happens immediately before your problem behavior is also important. Things that happen just before your behavior are called "antecedents." Antecedents can be internal events such as particular thoughts, feelings, or physical sensations. They can also be external events, such as interpersonal interactions, your own behavior, or even the use of drugs/alcohol. It will be important for you to learn what internal and external events trigger the behavior you want to work on changing.

Structured Diaries

You can use a diary to record the behavior you want to work on. A simple format for this diary is to set up three columns side by side for A (Antecedents), B (Behaviors), and C (Consequences).

Antecedents (A)	**Problem Behavior (B)**	**Consequences (C)**	**Working Hypothesis**
What situation are you in? In what context did the event take place? What were your thoughts, emotions, and	What did you do in terms of your behavior?	What effect did the problem behavior have on your emotions, physical sensations, and thoughts?	Looking at your ABC diary, make a note of your hypothesis as to what may be

physical sensations before the problem behavior?		What effect did the behavior have on other people?	maintaining your problem behavior.

Here are some examples of how someone else filled in this diary.

Antecedents (A)	Problem Behavior (B)	Consequences (C)	Working Hypothesis
What situation are you in? In what context did the event take place? What were your thoughts, emotions and physical sensations prior to the problem behavior?	What do you do in terms of your behavior?	What effect did the problem behavior have on your emotions, physical sensations, and thoughts? What effect did the behavior have on other people?	Looking at your ABC diary make a note of your hypothesis as to what may be maintaining your problem behavior.
My husband had just left the house to go to work and I was at home on my own. I was having the	I went to the fridge and got a bottle of wine out and sat and drank half	I felt less anxious and noticed the sick feeling in my stomach less.	Looking at my ABC, I can see that the consequences of drinking the wine were that it reduced my anxiety

thought that "I feel so lonely" and I felt anxious and had a sick feeling in my stomach.	of the bottle.		and uncomfortable physical sensations. I can see, therefore, that my wine drinking behavior is being *negatively reinforced.*

If you notice the outcome of your behavior is positive in some way, then this is likely to be reinforcing or maintaining your tendency to act in that particular way. For example, if you want to work on reducing a hair-pulling habit, you may notice that your C ("Consequences") column shows that you tend to feel less anxious or tense after pulling your hair. As this is a positive outcome, because it's nice to feel less anxious and tense, then you are likely to continue to behave in this way in similar situations in future.

Alternatively, if you notice that your C column shows that you are praised by your boss after engaging in the behavior in question in the B ("Behavior") column, then psychologists might say that your behavior is *positively reinforced.* Behaviors could be positively reinforced any time your behavior is immediately followed by sometime positive being added.

If your goal is to seek less reassurance at work, then you can record each episode of seeking reassurance. You will be able to see under what circumstances you seek reassurance from the "Antecedent" column. You will notice the key situations, thoughts, and feelings that come before and after seeking reassurance. This will allow you to start to stand back and work toward responding differently to these triggers.

If you want to work on a problem with overeating, you might notice from your self-monitoring diary that you only overeat when you are in a private setting alone or when feeling stressed.

To get control over your behavior, you need to identify what situations are associated with the behavior. There are no one-way streets in this process. Sometimes thoughts lead to feelings that lead to behaviors and other times behaviors lead to feelings and then to thoughts.

It is best to try and record things in your diary as soon as possible after the behavior occurred in order to get accurate information. Remember the purpose here is to find out which situations affect your behavior and what might be keeping you behaving in that particular way. Maintaining records allows you to act like a scientist to observe and reflect on the patterns of your behavior. Whatever pattern you observe from your self-monitoring will give important information about how to effect behavior change (Watson & Tharp, 2007).

Ideas for helping to change unwanted behavior:

Antecedents

Work on changing thoughts that come before problem behaviors by making use of the Thought Diary technique.

If physical symptoms tend to trigger the unwanted problem behavior, come up with a plan to managing these symptoms differently. For example, if a typical trigger for reassurance seeking is feelings of physical tension, you can develop a plan to managing these symptoms differently by practicing progressive muscle relaxation or doing some exercise.

Come up with some thoughts that motivate you to practice your alternative more helpful behaviors.

If a typical trigger is having an alcoholic drink, develop a plan for preventing yourself having access to alcohol.

Behaviors

Decide how you would like to behave differently in future situations. Put this in positive terms, so say what you would like to do instead of the unwanted behavior. For example, I would like to do some knitting with my hands rather than using my hands to pull out my hair. Alternatively, I would like to practice being assertive with my husband and requesting that he change his behavior rather than keeping quiet when he criticizes me.

Consequences

Come up with a way to reinforce your new, more helpful behaviors. It is essential to follow through with immediate positive reinforcement of your new goal behavior.

You could reinforce yourself for practicing the new helpful behavior by talking to yourself in a kind voice (*"Well done, John, that was a great step forward for you"*).

If appropriate, ask important people in your life to compliment you for changing your behavior.

You could agree with your partner or support person about the best way for them to respond when they notice you engage in your goal behavior.

You could make a list of the activities that you enjoy doing most and allow yourself to engage in one of these activities after you have practiced your new behavior.

Make sure you reinforce any new steps you take to behave in ways that resemble your goal behavior even if you don't fully achieve your new behavior. This will encourage you to continue to practice working toward new ideal goal behavior.

Assertiveness

Assertiveness is a technique that will allow you to communicate your needs directly to other people. You will, therefore, give yourself the best opportunity to have your needs met. Assertiveness can be learned just the same as any other skill. If you want to develop your assertiveness, you have to begin by understanding your rights and valuing yourself. It is imperative that you truly understand that your rights, your needs, your desires, your thoughts, and your feelings are just as important as anyone else's. Of course, the other side of this is that your feelings and thoughts are not any more important than anyone else's, as well. You have to believe that you truly deserve to be treated with respect and dignity, and you have to begin by no longer apologizing for everything.

Here is a chart to help you better understand the differences between passive, assertive, and aggressive thinking:

Passive	**Assertive**	**Aggressive**
Your thoughts do not matter as much as others	Your thoughts matter the same as others	Your thoughts matter more than others
Give in	Compromise	Take
Not talking	Talking and listening	Talking over others
Allowing others to bully you	Standing up for yourself	Bullying others
Not voicing your thoughts	Expressing your thoughts and feelings clearly	Being aggressive and loud, yelling your thoughts at others

To become more assertive, you have to develop your wants and your needs and you have to ask for them. You should not wait for another person to recognize what you want or what you need. You just might be waiting for a very long time. In order for you to perform to your best potential and to be your best self, you have to make sure that all of your needs are met. It is imperative that you find a way to get the things that you need without having to sacrifice other people in the process.

It is important to acknowledge that you are the only person responsible for your own behavior. You should not accept responsibility for how other people react to your statements because you cannot control anything other than yourself. So long as you do not violate the needs of anyone else you have just as much of a right to say what you think or to get what you need.

If you have negative thoughts or feelings, you should learn to express them in a healthy and positive fashion. You are absolutely allowed to be angry at the situation, but you still have to be respectful. You still have to control your emotions and, if you say what's on your mind, you have to do so in such a way that you don't outright hurt the feelings of anyone else. If someone is challenging your rights, you should stand up for yourself.

You are the one in control of your actions and your thoughts. You also have to allow yourself to make mistakes and to ask for help when you need it. This is a key component to being assertive. When you get feedback, you should not be angry or defensive about the comments you receive; instead, you should accept that feedback in a positive fashion. You don't have to agree with it but you should still be kind. Of course, you must also learn when to say no. You need to do what is right for you, especially if you are battling dependent personality disorder. It is important to understand that you cannot do everything and that you will never please everyone.

There are many ways in which you can practice communicating assertively, and you can adapt each of these tools to various situations in which you find yourself.

"I" statements.

Use phrases to convey your basic assertions such as I feel, I need, or I want.

Empathy

Recognize other people's viewpoints by stating something to the effect of:

"I understand this is difficult for you…when we meet friends you get very excited and want to tell them all your news."

And then express the things that you need

…"however, please can you try not to talk over me when we are socializing with friends?"

This is a wonderful assertiveness technique that you can use to make sure your needs are met.

One way to remain assertive is to use what is called the broken record technique. This technique means that you restate the message you are trying to convey using similar language until the person with whom you are speaking truly understands what it is you are trying to say. For example: If you cannot start a new project on your own right now and somebody close to you, such as a friend or family member, continues to ask that you start the project on your own, you can simply make it clear that you cannot begin any project on your own right now and you can use that statement over and over until the person gets the message.

This is a great way to protect yourself. You have to be sure that you protect your wants and your needs while remaining assertive and you have to prevent exploitation in order to do this. If you truly know that you will be unable to handle something in your current state, there's no shame in simply saying so and not allowing yourself to be put in an uncomfortable or undesirable situation.

Example: *Broken record technique*

Can you make sure that you start the project this afternoon?

I'm sorry, I can't start this until Joe returns from his holiday, as I need his input.

We need his project under way straight away.

I understand that this is an important project, but I can't start this until Joe gets back from his holiday, as his input is essential.

Joe is always away on holiday, just get going on it now.

Joe's input is essential to this project, so I can't start until he returns.

Another method for remaining assertive is to think through what you are going to say to the person before speaking to them. This will ensure you express the key points. You can use the prompts below to help.

Step 1: Begin by asking if now is a good time to have a conversation about the issue,

Is now an okay time to have a discussion about what happened when we met up with John and Pauline for coffee?

Step 2: Describe the issue and how you feel about it,

I felt hurt and upset when you put me down and belittled me in front of them.

Step 3: Tell the person what you need and how you anticipate feeling when they have made a change in their behavior.

I would feel very happy if you would not put me down in future, particularly when we are out socializing.

All of these skills can be learned and developed with time but like all things discussed in this book they must be practiced regularly and they will not happen overnight. One way to get in the habit of building your confidence in your assertiveness skills would be to create a list of situations during which you could practice.

Hierarchy of situations in which to practice being assertive	
Situation to practice	*Anticipated level of difficulty*
Being assertive with dad about how frequently I am willing to wash his clothes.	10/10
Telling Anna that I am not able to pick up her children from kindergarten.	9/10
Telling Frank that I am not willing to meet him for a coffee.	8/10
Being assertive with Jane about her always turning up late when we arrange to meet up.	7/10
Asking to be moved to a different room in a hotel.	6/10
Asking my son to stop asking me to invest in his latest business idea.	5/10
Asking for a refund of an item bought in a shop.	4/10

Now have a go at creating your own assertiveness practice plan.

Hierarchy of situations in which to practice being assertive	
Situation to practice	*Anticipated level of difficulty*

	10/10
	9/10
	8/10
	7/10
	6/10
	5/10
	4/10

Managing Unhelpful Reassurance Seeking

The impulse to seek reassurance from others often goes unnoticed. However, seeking excessive reassurance from other people will reduce your anxiety in the short term only. In the long term, seeking reassurance will typically maintain your anxiety and hold back your confidence in your ability to function independently. Therefore, resisting the demand for regular reassurance from other people is another important step in overcoming your anxiety.

The first step in managing unhelpful behaviors such as excessive reassurance seeking is to create a plan for yourself.

You can start by listing the specific behavior that you want to change. If you have family or friends that are close to you, it may be helpful to include them in your plan. You could ask your family member to comment positively when they see you doing things independently without asking for reassurance. If you are currently in therapy, you should share your plan with your therapist.

Once you have your plan, it is important that you set up the steps. The steps that you take are unique to your particular situation. Perhaps you become anxious or worried every time you think a work project is not perfect. In this case, you might normally ask for reassurance from work colleagues or family members. You may do this due to your anxiety telling you that it's going to turn out really badly and, in the worst case, you may end up being criticized or even losing your job. Catastrophic thinking can fuel your anxiety and increase your urge to seek reassurance from others. This would be a good opportunity to practice using the thought diary technique for identifying and challenging automatic thoughts that contribute to your anxiety and consider more helpful balance alternative thoughts.

While practicing your helpful alternative thoughts, it's important to act against what the anxiety motivates you to do by limiting or banning reassurance seeking. This is likely to feel uncomfortable initially but it will get easier with consistent practice. It's normal when making a change in your behavior to feel increased levels of anxiety in the short term. However, the longer you stick to your plan, the less you will feel the intense urge to seek reassurance and the less anxious you are likely to feel as you give yourself new opportunities to learn healthy ways of managing your anxiety.

It is important to remain consistent. This does not mean you should beat yourself up if things don't go as planned or you slip up now and again. It does, however, mean that you just need to put yourself back on track.

Learning to monitor your behavior change efforts can give you objective feedback on your progress and help you identify any roadblocks that are holding you back from change. A good first step would be to monitor every time you seek reassurance from other people and to focus particularly on the problem situations where you want to focus on reducing this behavior. We know that monitoring your behavior in this way will raise your awareness of this behavior and that in itself can help you to reduce it.

Problem Solving

Problem solving is part of evidence-based treatments for depression (Martell et al., 2010) and anxiety (Wilkinson et al., 2011). When human beings are struggling with mental health difficulties, we may not apply our problem-solving abilities systematically, meaning that practical issues remain in our life that can unintentionally fuel low mood or anxiety. People often worry in an attempt to solve practical problems. Unfortunately, worry is an inefficient form of problem solving that is associated with the negative side effects of anxiety and uncomfortable physical symptoms.

Working through a practical problem-solving worksheet is a quicker way of getting on top issues and can contribute to managing your mood. Common problems people face in life often revolve around: financial difficulties (being in debt), unemployment, having too many tasks to do, and relationship problems (such as arguments with your partner). Follow the practical steps below to start addressing unresolved problems going on in your life.

Step 1: Define the problem you face clearly

Write down the problem you face in a way that is clear enough to be tackled. Try to break the problem down into the simplest smallest step possible. Try to solve only one problem at a time.

Step 2: Brainstorm as many different solutions as possible

Don't discount any of the potential solutions that come to mind. The more solutions you come up with, the better. If someone you cared about came to you with this practical problem, what advice would you give them? Write down all the solutions you come up with.

Step 3: Consider the advantages and disadvantages of each solution

Example – My husband and I keep arguing		
Solution	*Advantages*	*Disadvantages*
Talk to him about engaging in couples marital therapy appointments.	We could talk over our issues with the help of a trained counselor to see if we can get on top of them.	He may react badly or refuse to give the counseling a go. It might be expensive to see a counselor.
Divorce him.	We won't have to argue anymore.	I love him and don't want us to break up.
Book some pleasant activities for us to engage in together.	This will give us some opportunities to engage in enjoyable activities and relieve some of the tension.	We might disagree on what activities to try together.
Ignore the problem and see if it resolves itself.	It won't require any effort or discomfort on my part.	I've already been ignoring it for the last six months and it hasn't improved yet.

Step 4: Pick one of the solutions

Consider the advantages and disadvantages of each solution and pick one that looks best overall. Make sure the solution that you pick is practical and within your own control to achieve.

Step 5: List the specific steps you will need to go through in order to carry out the chosen solution

What, specifically, are you going to do?

When, specifically, are you going to do it?

What resources will you need in order to carry out each step?

Step 6: Try out your plan

Make sure that you put a date in your diary for when you are going to return to the problem to see whether or not it has been resolved by your chosen solution. This may be in a week or in several weeks' time, depending on how long it takes you to carry out the steps you have identified.

Step 7: Review the outcome

Did it help you address the problem? Maybe the problem was completely resolved, in which case it's time to give yourself a pat on the back. May be it was only partially resolved or completely unresolved. In this case, return to Step 2 and again work your way through the other steps. Continue this circular process until you have managed to resolve the issue you are faced with.

If you experience difficulties working through your issue, it may be because you are trying to address more than one problem at a time. If this is the case, break the issue down into manageable steps rather than trying to solve everything all at once, as this is likely to leave you feeling overwhelmed.

Things to Remember

- To become more assertive, you have to develop your wants and your needs and you have to ask for them.
- It is important to acknowledge that you are the only person responsible for your own behavior.
- If you have negative thoughts or feelings, you should learn to express them in a healthy and positive fashion.
- One way to remain assertive is to use the broken record technique.
- A structured diary is where you keep records of your targets or the change you want to achieve, the consequences of it, and the antecedents. You want to record all three (antecedents, behaviors, and consequences) so that you can keep track of your efforts. You should keep in your journal a record of the thoughts you have too. This will help you to uncover the negative automatic thoughts that haunt you, even if you don't realize they are there.
- It is best that you record thoughts and actions as soon as they occur.

Chapter Eight: Tips for Family Members Living with a Person with a Dependent Personality Disorder

If someone in your family has a dependent personality disorder, it can be a challenge to live with them and provide them with the support they request without losing yourself in that task.

You may feel that you are doing them a favor if you offer to do tasks for them that they are anxious about. However, in the long term, this is likely to increase their dependence on you and prevent them from building confidence in their own ability to do things for themselves. You may also feel that taking over responsibility for part of your relative's life is in their best interest. You may feel that you are under a lot of pressure to help out in this way. However, in the long run, this is unlikely to be particularly helpful. In the same way, your relative my make anxious demands of you to make important life decisions for them. It's important that you encourage them to make their own decisions.

Make sure that you comment positively on any small positive changes you notice in your relative's behavior. Any time they make small improvements, such as making a small decision for themselves, reward them immediately in a way that they will find encouraging. You know your relative best. If they would find a smile and a hug from you a reward for making a positive change in their behavior, make sure you give it to them.

Have a discussion with your relative about the key problems and goals they have decided to work on. Ask your relative if there is any way that you can help them regularly practice the strategies outlined in this book.

It may take a significant length of time for your relative to make changes and learn to express their thoughts and feelings more regularly, and that is okay. At home, families can help by discussing your relative's goals and making sure they are small and achievable.

As a family member living with someone who has dependent personality disorder, it is imperative that you educate yourself as much as you can about the disorder and the available treatments. The more you know, the more you can help; having some understanding of why a person reacts the way they do can help provide the patience necessary to move that person in the right direction.

To live with a person who has dependent personality disorder, it is imperative that you remain mindful of their situation, so that you can step back from any situation or event in the moment and remind yourself of where this person is coming from and what burden they are trying to alleviate.

It is important to talk to your loved ones about the things they love. Try to keep your loved one involved in activities they enjoy. Integrate activities such as regular exercise, balanced and healthy meals, and stress-reducing activities like painting or yoga. Be alert for the possibility of any substance abuse symptoms; if you notice these, encourage your loved one to get treatment.

Avoid using negative language, especially when your loved one is around. Instead of telling them they are "too dependent" on others, explain instead that "becoming more independent will make you improve your self-confidence." Encourage them to consider engaging in psychological therapy such as CBT by explaining how it could help, and insist that they deserve to build their confidence and get more out of life.

CBT is an effective treatment for a wide range of mental health problems that can be personalized for whatever works best for the individual. Seeking out CBT is best done when complications arise from the dependent personality disorder such as phobias, depression, anxiety disorders, or substance abuse. Getting help early can prevent additional complications.

It can be difficult for those who are anxious to seek help due to the fear that discussing their problems could damage their relationships. It is because of this inherent fear that family members should help their loved ones recognize that they have a problem and that talking about it is likely to further improve rather than harm their relationships.

Family members can encourage their loves ones to seek out group therapy in tandem with CBT as a way of learning how to be assertive and to acquire problem-solving skills in a group dynamic. For those who are insecure or uncomfortable with one-on-one sessions, the group therapy environment can provide encouragement in a complementary form by way of discussions with people in similar situations.

Family or couples counseling is particularly helpful for those who are living with someone who has dependent personality disorder. Such counseling is meant to tend to the relationship between family members by having all members in the same room. This provides the opportunity to cultivate empathy for one another, build upon existing strengths, and make positive changes all around. It can be a useful place to learn new skills, such as conflict management or negotiation. For someone in a relationship with a person who has dependent personality disorder, couples counseling can help to reduce any existing anxiety in the relationship, by assigning homework tasks for the couple to consider at home, the results of which are discussed at the following sessions. These homework assignments are crucial in building the relationship or repairing it. Many couples benefit from doing some self-help reading (Beck, 1988).

Chapter Nine: How to Get Professional Treatment

If you are in need of professional treatment, you can get the help you need from a CBT therapist by searching for therapists in your local area certified under BABCP for the U.K. (http://www.babcp.com/) and the Academy of Cognitive Therapy for the U.S. (http://www.academyofct.org/).

It is recommended that, when searching for help, you find a qualified and certified professional with a level of training and experience that you prefer. Not all therapists are alike, and you may find, after some preliminary sessions, that one works out better for you than others.

CBT Self-Help Websites

Below you will find a handful of CBT self-help websites where you can access books and online resources.

U.S.-based Beck Institute:

https://www.beckinstitute.org/

U.K. Oxford Cognitive Therapy Centre:

https://www.octc.co.uk/

Mood Gym for online CBT skills training:

https://moodgym.anu.edu.au/

U.K. National Health Service guidelines:

http://www.nhs.uk/conditions/stress-anxiety-depression/pages/self-help-therapies.aspx

Self-help book series using CBT techniques:

http://www.overcoming.co.uk/

Free online CBT training—Living Life to the Full:

http://www.llttf.com/

U.S. Albert Ellis Institute:

http://albertellis.org/

Things to Remember

- As a family member living with someone who has dependent personality disorder, it is imperative that you educate yourself as much as you can about the disorder and the available treatments.
- Seeking out therapy is best when complications arise from the dependent personality disorder, such as phobias, depression, anxiety disorders, or substance abuse. Getting help early can prevent additional complications.
- Family or couples counseling can be helpful for those who are living with someone who has dependent personality disorder.

References

American Psychiatric Association. (2013). *Diagnostic and statistical manual of mental disorders* (5th ed.). Arlington, VA: Author.

Beck, A.T., Rush, A.J., Shaw, B.F., & Emery, G. (1979). *Cognitive therapy of depression.* New York: Guilford Press.

Beck, A.T. (1988). *Love is never enough.* New York: Harper & Row.

Beck, A.T., Freeman, A., & Associates. (2015). *Cognitive therapy of personality disorders* (3rd ed.). New York: Guilford Press.

Centers for Disease Control. (1992, September 16). Serious mental illness and disability in the adult household population: United

States, 1989. *Advance Data* No. 218 from *Vital and Health Statistics,* National Center for Health Statistics. : A Self-presentational view of psychotherapy. *Psychological Bulletin,* 126, 475-494.

Cowen, P., Harrison, P., & Burns, T. (2012). *Shorter Oxford textbook of psychiatry.* Oxford: Oxford University Press.

Dryden, W. (2009). *Understanding Emotional Problems: The REBT Perspective.* London: Routledge.

Grant, B. F., Stinson, F.S., Dawson, D.A., Chou, S.P., Ruan, W.J., & Pickering, R.P. (2004). Co-occurrence of 12-month alcohol and drug use disorders and personality disorders in the United States: Results from the National Epidemiologic Survey on Alcohol and Related Conditions. *Archives of General Psychiatry, 61*(4), 361-368.

Martell, C.R., Dimidjian, S., & Herman-Dunn, R. (2010). *Behavioral activation for depression: A clinician's guid*e. New York: Guilford Press.

Mayne, T.J., Norcross, J.C., & Sayette, M.A. (1994). Admission requirements, acceptance rates, and financial assistance in clinical psychology programs. *American Psychologist,* 49, 806-811.

National Institute of Mental Health. (1982). *Television and behavior: Ten years of scientific progress and implications for the eighties.* Washing, DC: U.S. Government Printing Office.

Padesky, C., & Beck, J. (2015). Avoidant personality disorder. In A. Beck, D. Davis, & A. Freeman (Eds.), *Cognitive therapy of personality disorders* (3rd ed., pp. 174-202). New York: Guilford.

Robins, L., & Regier, D. (Eds.). (1991). *Psychiatric disorders in America.* New York: Free Press.

Sperry, L., & Sperry, J. (2016). *Cognitive behavior therapy of DSM-5 personality disorders.* New York: Routledge.

Sungur, M.Z., Gündüz, A. (2015). Histrionic Personality Disorder. In A. Beck, D. Davis, & A. Freeman (Eds.), *Cognitive therapy of personality disorders* (3rd ed., pp. 325-345). New York: Guilford.

Veale, D., & Willson, R. (2007). *Manage Your Mood: How to use behavioral activation techniques to overcome depression.* London: Robinson.

Watson, D.L., & Tharp, R.G. (2007). *Self-directed behavior.* Belmont: Thomson.

Wilkinson, A., Meares, K., Freeston, M. (2011). *CBT for worry & generalised anxiety disorder.* London: Sage.

CPSIA information can be obtained
at www.ICGtesting.com
Printed in the USA
BVHW02s1926041117
499536BV00019B/449/P

9 780995 561007